商务英语报刊选读

（第2版）

Selected Business English Readings from Newspapers and Magazines

（Second Edition）

主 编 董晓波

清华大学出版社
北京交通大学出版社
·北京·

内容简介

本书旨在对学习者进行全面而严格的商务英语基础理论教育及英语语言技能培训，让学习者在阅读和理解商务英语文章的基础上，既能学习丰富的商务知识，又能熟悉一些商务方面的英语表达，以便提高跨文化商务交际水平。

本书适用于商务英语专业的学生，同时也适合作对外经贸、财政金融、工商管理等专业的教材，还可作为从事国际商务经贸工作人员的重要参考资料。

本书封面贴有清华大学出版社防伪标签，无标签者不得销售。
版权所有，侵权必究。侵权举报电话：010-62782989 13501256678 13801310933

图书在版编目（CIP）数据

商务英语报刊选读 / 董晓波主编. —2版. —北京：北京交通大学出版社：清华大学出版社，2017.9（2022.6重印）
ISBN 978-7-5121-1611-5

Ⅰ.①商… Ⅱ.①董… Ⅲ.①商务—英语—阅读教学—自学参考资料 Ⅳ.①F7

中国版本图书馆CIP数据核字（2017）第235441号

商务英语报刊选读
SHANGWU YINGYU BAOKAN XUANDU

策划编辑：	郭东青
责任编辑：	郭东青
出版发行：	清 华 大 学 出 版 社　邮编：10084　电话：010-62776969
	北京交通大学出版社　邮编：10044　电话：010-51686414
印　刷　者：	艺堂印刷（天津）有限公司
经　　　销：	全国新华书店
开　　　本：	203 mm×280 mm　印张：15.75　字数：331千字
版　　　次：	2017年9月第2版　2022年6月第4次印刷
书　　　号：	ISBN 978-7-5121-1611-5/F·1727
印　　　数：	7 001～9 500册　定价：39.00元

本书如有质量问题，请向北京交通大学出版社质监组反映。对您的意见和批评，我们表示欢迎和感谢。
投诉电话：010-51686043，51686008；传真：010-62225406；E-mail：press@bjtu.edu.cn。

第 2 版前言 Preface

《商务英语报刊选读》是"通识教育系列丛书"之一，第1版上市后，受到了广大教师和学习者积极肯定的评价。我也经常收到全国各地使用此教材的老师们的邮件。随着全球经济一体化和中国对外开放的进一步扩大，中国正以更快的步伐融入全球化的浪潮中。我国日益频繁的对外商务交往需要培养大量英语基础扎实、同时精通国际商贸知识的高素质的复合型商务英语人才。《商务英语报刊选读》一书能够为中国商务英语人才的培养略尽绵薄之力，我感到由衷的高兴。

高校商务英语的人才培养主要目的是让学生熟练应用商务英语，而单纯的语言练习不能满足这种需要。《商务英语报刊选读》的宗旨是培养专业的商务英语人才，使他们向通晓国际经贸基本知识和实务的方向发展，成为具有较强沟通能力、应用能力和较高综合素质的复合型商务英语专门人才。

《商务英语报刊选读》第2版充分考虑市场需求并广泛吸取各方建议，以提高学生的语言技能，在第1版的基础上，以扩充专业知识，培养应用能力为宗旨，对部分章节予以压缩、更新，将第1版的15个单元，压缩成为更精华的11个单元；选取目前最热门的商务话题，完善部分单词和注释，更新部分内容，突出时代性和实用性，从而更好地满足教师和学习者的需要，充分发挥语言实践课教材的作用。

本书可供普通高等院校商务英语专业学生使用，还可供具有一定英语水平的从事国际商务工作以及其他社会各界专业人士学习参考。

本书在修订过程中，学生肖婷、陈柳华协助整理书稿、补充资料，在此表示感谢。由于时间仓促，本书在编写过程中难免存在不足之处，望读者和专家们不吝赐教。

编　者
2017年5月

前言 Preface

随着全球经济一体化、中国对外开放的进一步扩大，中国社会需要大量英语基础好，又熟悉商务贸易知识的复合型人才。改革开放三十多年以来，我国综合国力显著提升，经济对外开放与融合的程度不断加深。大型企业向国际化管理模式的转变及工商企业走出去战略的实施，对商务英语专业人才培养模式提出了更高的要求。从外语教育的角度来看，商务英语专业学生除了需要具有扎实的语言基本功底外，同时还需要具备较强的跨文化商务交际能力。为满足各大专院校培养复合型商务英语人才及社会上各阶层经济贸易工作者进一步学习和提高的需要，我们特编写了《商务英语报刊选读》一书。

阅读是语言学习者最重要的信息输入形式之一，本书全面而概括地介绍了商务领域的各个关键领域，如企业管理、市场营销、电子商务等。本书旨在对学习者进行全面而严格的商务基础理论教育及英语语言技能的培训，让学习者在阅读和理解商务英语文章的基础上，既能学习丰富的商务知识，又能熟悉一些商务方面的英语表达，以便提高跨文化商务交际水平。全书共十五个单元，每单元内容主要由两篇精读文章、一篇补充材料及课后练习组成。

本书编写具有以下特点。

1. 选材新颖，针对性强，全书用文遴选自国内外的主要报纸、杂志，包括《经济学家》(*The Economist*)、《金融时报》(*Financial Times*)、《财富》(*Fortune*)、《华尔街日报》(*The Wall Street Journal*)、《哈佛商业评论》(*Harvard Business Review*)、《中国日报》(*China Daily*)、《北京周报》(*Beijing Review*) 等。内容基本能够反映世界商务和贸易发展的主流和大趋势，具有时代性、知识性和趣味性。

2. 设计科学，简明易懂。每篇精读文章均有导读帮助理解主旨，且文章后皆有生词短语列表、专业术语、背景知识的注释，另每单元最后附有tips板块，补充商务领域知识，以便提高读者的阅读和学习效率。

3. 本书配有相应的图表，确保阐述清晰，增加学习的趣味性。

4. 每单元的两篇精读文章后均有练习题，帮助学习者迅速掌握要点，巩固对专业知识的运用和把握。

本书适用于商务英语专业的学生，同时也适用于对外经贸、财政金融、工商管理等专业的学生，也可作为从事国际商务经贸工作的人员的重要参考资料。

本书由董晓波任主编，陈艳、蒋菲、王雪任副主编，华黎、王辰诚、郑欣参编。在整个编写过程中，我们虽力求完美，但由于水平所限，不乏疏漏和欠妥之处，恳请广大同人和读者不吝指正，以便充实与完善。

编　者

2012 年 11 月

Contents

Unit 1　Capital Markets ·· 1
　Text A　Banking Industry ··· 1
　Text B　Stock Exchange ··· 10
　Supplementary Reading
　　American Stock Markets—Reversal of Fortune ·· 18
Unit 2　International Marketing ··· 22
　Text A　Business Planning—Marketing Planning ··· 22
　Text B　Supporting Offline Campaign Launches with Online Marketing ············· 30
　Supplementary Reading
　　Online-coupon Firms—Groupon Anxiety ·· 36
Unit 3　Business Elite ·· 42
　Text A　The Resurrection of Steve Jobs
　　　　　—That Which Does Not Kill the Boss of Apple Seems to Make Him
　　　　　　Stronger ·· 42
　Text B　Ann Moore:The CEO of Time ·· 48
　Supplementary Reading
　　Steve Jobs and the iPad of Hope
　　　—Apple's Innovation Machine Churns out Another Game-changing Device ······ 53
Unit 4　E-Commerce ·· 62
　Text A　In E-Commerce, More Is More ··· 62
　Text B　The Alibaba E-Commerce Empire ··· 69

Supplementary Reading

Online Shopping: Selling Becomes Sociable ·· 75

Unit 5　Economic Globalization and Multinational Corporation ············· 80

Text A　Globalization vs. Economic Sovereignty ·· 80

Text B　The World's Top Choice

——China Remains the Most Popular Destination for Foreign Direct

Investment ·· 88

Supplementary Reading

McDonald's Eyes Growing Presence in Local Market ······························ 93

Unit 6　Economic Regulations and Law ··· 98

Text A　U.S. Sets 21st Century Goal: Building a Better Patent Office ·················· 98

Text B　Anti-Trust Law Treats "All Firms Equally" over 140 Cases Handled: Rules

in Line with International Principles ··· 105

Supplementary Reading

China E-Commerce Giant Launches Campaign to Fight Online Piracy ········· 112

Unit 7　Human Resources Management ··· 118

Text A　Capturing the State of Human Resources in an Annual Report ·············· 118

Text B　The Tech Effect on Human Resources ··· 127

Supplementary Reading

Risk Management and Human Resources Team up to Cut Absence Costs ····· 134

Unit 8　Advertising and Publicity ··· 145

Text A　Internet Advertising ·· 145

Text B　Beijing Tries to Push Beyond "Made in China" ································· 151

Supplementary Reading

The Harder Hard Sell ··· 160

Unit 9　Training ··· 173

Text A　Training the Trainer ·· 173

Text B　Training Needs Assessment: A Must for Developing an Effective Training

Program ··· 181

Supplementary Reading

    An Innovative Method for Role-specific Quality-training Evaluation······················191

Unit 10   Corporate Culture ···198

Text A   What Is Corporate Culture? ··198

Text B   Four Steps to Go Green Like eBay—Starting with Employees ····················206

Supplementary Reading

    The Fall of a Corporate Queen ··212

Unit 11   Business Ethics and Corprate Social Responsibility ····························219

Text A   The Corporate Responsibility Commitment ··219

Text B   Controversial Chemical Poses Challenge for Colgate-Palmolive ····················226

Supplementary Reading

    Toyota Recall: Five Critical Lessons ··235

Unit 1

Capital Markets

Text A Banking Industry

> 导读：银行是经营货币和信用业务的金融机构，通过发行信用货币、管理货币流通、调剂资金供求、办理货币存贷与结算，充当信用的中介人。银行是现代金融业的主体，是国民经济运转的枢纽。在国际贸易和繁多的金融业务中，银行扮演着重要的角色。

Banks satisfy simple wants. People with more money than is needed deposit it into banks for safekeeping. While on deposit, the money is utilized by others. "embarking on enterprises beyond their own means," says Dunbar. The bank's role is to manage the lender's risk, ensuring his money is available when he wants it back. The lenders are compensated through the payment of interest.

Banks raise funds through the stock exchange, depositors' funds, and interest on loans, lending to and borrowing from each other, and trading financial instruments. The Central Bank owns, prints and distributes money. Bank types include mom-and-pop retail banks, which offer savings accounts, loans and credit cards, as well as commercial and merchant banks dealing with large and small businesses. Riskier investment banks put their funds in more speculative, volatile money and equity markets.

Commercial banks are licensed to conduct banking operations within their local communities. All commercial banks possess the same overall functions granted to them in accordance with their banking licenses. They are able to take deposits, make loans, own securities and conduct banking services for their clients. They must also represent the areas where they are located. This separates them from the very large central and international banks. Since commercial banks are profit-based organizations that are privately owned, they must be effective in serving the financial needs of their customers.

Marketing Strategies for the Banking Industry

Banks have a high level of competition, and effective marketing can have a large impact on consumers who are choosing new services. As you develop a marketing campaign for your bank, consider how you can work with customers at all stages of their financial planning to make their banking experience stress-free and convenient.

Education

One of the most common pitfalls for banking customers is a lack of knowledge about how they should handle their money. As a bank, you are immediately in a position of expertise; use that expertise to help educate a potential customer base. Start by targeting people who might need financial help: soon-to-be college graduates or people with a history of credit problems, for example. Spread the word about your bank and help create awareness about banking options by holding community education sessions, publishing a "Banking 101" blog, or volunteering to speak at colleges about financial planning for young professionals.

Peace of Mind

When customers fall on hard times or when they face an economic downturn, finances become a top concern. Banks can gain a market advantage by using strategies that create peace of mind for their customers. You might offer special accounts with low monthly fees, for example, or design a program that will help keep track of bills and spending each month. To attract customers who are worried about their finances, use an emotional appeal that is designed to convince them that with your financial services, everything will be okay; everything from the wording of your advertisement and website copy to the demeanor of your customers service associates can be part of a marketing strategy that calms and reassures customers.

Convenience

Modern consumers are busy and accustomed to the ease of handling their business online. Make your bank a natural choice by marketing the convenience of using your services. If you offer a banking application for a mobile phone, promote it heavily in your online and offline advertisements, and include direct download links from your website. Update your systems to allow digital deposits or offer a pick-up service for deposits from business customers. If you operate mainly with in-person business, make your bankers part of the program by helping them conduct quick, friendly transactions that do not require much time or effort on the part of the consumer; focus marketing materials on you convenient locations and low-effort banking.

Ease of Comparison

When consumers set out to choose a bank or a banking service, it is easy to become overwhelmed by the amount of choices that are available. To make your bank more approachable, focus your marketing efforts on the ease of comparison between products. You might use marketing materials that talk about the different types of accounts, make recommendations based on where customers are in their lives, or target special-needs consumers like frequent international travelers or new parents. In doing so, you can let your customers know that you can help them choose an account that is right for their needs.

Banking Industry Problems

The recession of 2008—2009 exposed several problems in the banking industry. In addition to numerous bank closings, funds used by the Federal Depositors Insurance Corp

(FDIC) to insure bank deposits shrank by 40 percent, representing billions of dollars. Some of the problems in the banking industry can be traced to the type of loans they were making.

Failed Banks

Dozens of banks failed in 2008 and 2009, many of whom were heavy into commercial real estate loans, construction loans and land loans. Commercial real estate loans finance the strip malls and shopping malls that saw decreasing numbers of customers as the economy declined. Owners were not able to make the payments and may have abandoned the property, leaving the banks on the hook. This led to undercapitalization at many banks, which caused them to be taken over by the FDIC.

Sub Prime Lending

Many banks engaged in sub-prime mortgage lending. These loans were made to customers who did not qualify for standard mortgage loans because of weak credit, insufficient income or an unstable job situation. A sub-prime customer is much riskier because of these factors. Many loans made to these customers were adjustable rate mortgages, which are tied to certain indexes, plus a margin, that increase periodically and raise the mortgage payment. Some customers saw their payments increase by hundreds of dollars, making them unaffordable. Foreclosures reached record levels when homeowners could not make these payments.

Foreclosures

The increase in foreclosures caused the value of homes to decline substantially. Many homeowners were left owing more than their homes were worth. Faced with foreclosure, they also were unable to sell the homes without going through a short sale, which potentially could leave them owing a deficiency balance. The increase in foreclosures also caused a decrease in demand for housing.

Bad Loans

Some banks made a lot of bad loans. Many customers should not have been approved for loans in the first place. Other banks invested in risky mortgage-backed securities. Then, when the recession hit, many people lost their jobs and were unable to make loan payments. Delinquency rates for mortgage loans soared, as did losses and bad debts.

Reserve Requirements

A lot of banks didn't have sufficient reserves. This is the portion of customers' deposits that banks are required to keep on hand, in the cash vault or on deposit with the Federal Reserve. These reserves help offset losses and assist with everyday banking transactions. When banks don't have enough reserves, they cannot lend money until the reserves are replenished. Banks can borrow from other banks at the Fed Funds rate, which is 0.25 percent. These types of loans are usually overnight borrowing.

SWOT Analysis of Banking Industry

SWOT analyses take into account the strengths, weaknesses, opportunities and threats facing a business, organization or operation, in terms of serving customers, stakeholders and their own employees. A SWOT analysis of the banking industry will list these four components and illustrate for executives and management the areas the 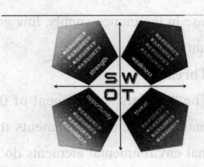 industry is performing well in not so well in. The SWOT also highlights the areas where there is opportunity to develop further and areas where there is potential to be hurt in the future.

Strengths

The "Strengths" portion of the banking industry's SWOT analysis is a list of the internal operational elements where the banking industry is succeeding or excelling. These elements need to refer to features the industry can control and has a direct power to change. For example, the banking industry's strengths can include record-high annual returns, diversified investment portfolio offerings, decreases in transaction and trading fees, an increase in the number of ATM machines and increased market share.

Weaknesses

The "Weaknesses" element of the banking industry's SWOT analysis is a list of the internal operational elements the banking industry needs to improve upon. These elements need to refer to features the industry can control and has a direct power to change. For example, the banking industry's weaknesses can include high loan rates, low bond credit ratings, an increased number of outstanding junk bonds, an increase in loan-sharking activity and an increased number of high-risk investment options.

Opportunities

The "Opportunities" part of the banking industry's SWOT analysis is a list of the external environmental elements the banking industry can potentially take advantage of in the near future or long-term. These external environmental elements should not reflect the internal components of the industry, but rather the factors or features outside the industry's control. For example, the banking industry's opportunities can include a growing economy, banking deregulation, increased client borrowing, an increase in the number of banks, an increase in the money supply, low government-set credit rates and larger customer checking account balances.

Threats

The "Threats" component of the banking industry's SWOT analysis is a list of the external environmental elements that can potentially harm the banking industry. These external environmental elements do not reflect the internal components of the industry, but the factors or features outside the industry's control. For example, the banking industry's threats could include a declining economy, increased banking regulations, larger capital gains taxes, new high-risk investment vehicles or higher health care costs. It's important to realize these examples are not black and white. For example, "new high-risk investment vehicles" are inherently a liability because they include increased risk, but depending on the financial stake and position, it could be an opportunity or threat.

Designing the SWOT Analysis Chart

SWOT analyses feature a two-by-two chart, where one of the four topics is listed in one of the four boxes. Strengths and weaknesses appear in the top row, with the strengths on the left and weaknesses on the right. Opportunities and threats appear in the bottom row, with opportunities on the left and threats on the right.

Notes:

1. Central bank（中央银行）: A central bank, reserve bank, or monetary authority is a public institution that usually issues the currency, regulates the money supply, and controls the interest rates in a country. Central banks often also oversee the commercial banking system of their respective counties. In contrast to a commercial bank, a central bank possesses a monopoly on printing the national currency, which usually serves as the nation's legal tender.

The primary function of a central bank is to provide the nation's money supply, but more active duties include controlling interest rates and acting as a lender of last resort to the banking sector during times of financial crisis. It may also have supervisory powers, to ensure that banks and other financial institutions do not behave recklessly or fraudulently.

2. Savings account（储蓄账户）: Savings accounts are accounts maintained by retail financial institutions that pay interest but cannot be used directly as money (for example, by writing a cheque). These accounts let customers set aside a portion of their liquid assets while earning a monetary return.

3. sub-prime mortgage（次贷按揭）: In finance, sub-prime lending (also referred to as near-prime, non-prime, and second-chance lending) means making loans to people who may have difficulty maintaining the repayment schedule, sometimes reflecting setbacks, such as unemployment, divorce, medical emergencies, etc.

Words & Expressions:

1. speculative [ˈspekjulətiv] *adj.* 投机的；推测的；思索性的
2. volatile [ˈvɔlətail] *adj.* [化学]挥发性的；不稳定的；爆炸性的；
   反复无常的
   n. 挥发物；有翅的动物

3. pitfall ['pitfɔ:l] n. 陷阱，圈套；缺陷；诱惑
4. index ['indeks] n. 指标；指数；索引；指针
   vi. 做索引
   vt. 指出；编入索引中
5. margin ['mɑ:dʒin] n. 边缘；利润，余裕；页边的空白
   vt. 加边于；加旁注于
6. deficiency [di'fiʃənsi] n. 缺陷，缺点；缺乏；不足的数额
7. foreclosure [fɔ:'kləuʒə] n. 丧失抵押品赎回权
8. delinquency [di'liŋkwənsi] n. 行为不良，违法犯罪；失职，怠工
9. replenish [ri'pleniʃ] vt. 补充，再装满；把……装满；给……添加燃料
10. portfolio [pɔ:t'fəuljəu] n. 公文包；文件夹；证券投资组合；部长职务
11. deregulation [ˌdi:ˌregju'leiʃn] n. 违反规定，反常；撤销管制规定
12. liability [ˌlaiə'biləti] n. 责任；债务；倾向

Exercises:

I. Fill in the blanks with the suitable words or expressions given in the box. Change the form when necessary.

| liability | portfolio | speculative | in accordance with | margin |

1. There is little doubt that adding some volatility insurance to your _____ is a good idea.
2. Some analysts doubt that the unit can ever regain a 20 percent _____.
3. However, the foundation dismissed the speculation, insisting that the tests were conducted _____ professional standards.
4. _____ borrowers can meet current interest payments from cash flows but need to "roll over" their debt in order to pay back the principal.
5. Insured can select Limit of _____ and currency for coverage.

II. Translate the following phrases into Chinese or English.

1. retail bank
2. equity market
3. bad loan
4. delinquency rate
5. banking deregulation
6. 中央银行
7. 营销策略
8. 垃圾债券
9. 自动提款机
10. SWOT 分析（优势、劣势、机会、威胁）

III. Read the following text and fill in the blanks with the words given in the box.

| dealing | rates | whatever | achieved | blaming |
| improvement | denial | struggle | acceptance | repay |

(1) _____ with Sovereign debt is like dealing with grief; the five stages of (2) _____, anger, bargaining, depression and (3) _____. The denial stage lasts quite a long time; arguably Portugal is still in it. Governments will say they don't have a problem, their banks are fine, their debt-to-GDP ratio is quite low or (4) _____. When the markets ignore these bromides and push yields higher, governments move to the next stage-anger-(5) _____ the speculators in the form of hedge funds or the rating agencies that don't understand the accounts. Bargaining has followed in both countries as the Irish and Greeks have turned to their EU neighbours for help. They have received funding at better (6) _____ than they could have (7) _____ on the markets, but it is still debt that they will (8) _____ to pay back. Depression might follow as they realize they face years of austerity without much sign of (9) _____. The acceptance stage will then be reached when these countries realize they can't afford to (10) _____ these debts and so they won't.

Text B　Stock Exchange

> 导读：证券交易所是依据国家有关法律，经政府证券主管机关批准设立的集中进行证券交易的有形场所。通过股票的发行，大量的资金流入股市，又流入了发行股票的企业，促进了资本的集中，提高了企业资本的有机构成，大大加快了商品经济的发展。若要在股票市场中进行有效投资，不仅要对股票市场进行潜心研究，还要具备对整个经济前景敏锐的洞察力。

The Stock Exchange is not actually one single unit, but a general name for multiple exchanges throughout the world. These exchanges handle the buying and selling of securities and financial paper. How did Stock Exchanges begin and what is their role in today's world?

Identification

The stock exchange is also known as a share market. Stock exchanges are usually a corporation or other mutual organization providing facilities for stock brokers and traders to buy and sell securities and stocks. Each stock exchange usually has a central facility, mainly for bookkeeping, where transactions and trades are recorded. The stock exchange is the central component to stock markets.

While a great portion of securities and paper are handled through the stock exchanges, not all of it is. The trading which is handled outside of an exchange is called "off exchange" or "over-the-counter." Most bonds are handled outside of the stock exchange community.

The first major stock exchange was the New York Stock Exchange. It was founded in 1792 by 24 New York stockbrokers and merchants. There are two basic types of stock exchanges. The face-to-face exchange is what most people thing of. Here, orders are sent through brokerage firms to a trading floor where a floor broker walks over to a specialist who helps him buy and sell the stock. The New York Stock Exchange is a face-to-face exchange. The NASDAQ is an over-the-counter (OTC) exchange. Here, there is no central location, and all trading is done through a computer network.

The four most famous, and important, exchanges are the New York Stock Exchange, the NASDAQ, the London Stock Exchange, and the Honk Kong Stock Exchange.

Benefits

For any one corporation to buy or sell shares or stocks it must be listed on the stock exchange. For a corporation to be listed on an exchange, it must first become a member of that exchange. Individual shareholders do not need to be members of any stock exchange to buy and sell shares of listed corporations.

While shares and stocks are what the stock exchanges are known for, there are other securities which are sold as well. Other transactions can include payments of income or dividends, unit trusts or other mutual investments and bonds.

History

It is commonly thought that the idea of the stock exchange began in the middle of the 13th century. Venetian bankers had begun to trade government securities. In the late 13th century commodity traders began to gather at a house in Bruges. This meeting became known as the "Bruges Bourse" or Bruges Purse. Commodities trading soon spread to Flanders, Ghent and Amsterdam; while government securities trading spread from Venice to Verona, Genoa, and Flanders in modern day Italy by the 14th century.

The Dutch would later join the trend and start companies which allowed shareholders to invest in business ventures and share in the profits and losses. In 1602, at the Amsterdam Stock Exchange, the first shares of the Dutch East India Company were traded. This would be followed by the opening of the London Stock Exchange in 1688.

Function

The Stock Exchanges of the world play multiple roles in the economics and economy. This includes such issues as raising capital for business expansion; moving savings into investment; facilitating the growth of companies by merger agreements and takeovers using the stock market as a means of financing. It also includes distribution of assets and profits of a business; providing for corporate governance through shareholders; allowing smaller investors to purchase and sell stocks; selling government issue bonds to help government fund projects and being a barometer to the economy by providing a record of shares bought or sold and how fast.

Geography

While most people are aware of the stock exchange in their respective country, the concept of one single Stock Exchange is misleading. There are several Stock Exchanges which conduct business daily, and usually interact. If one exchange begins to see a significant shift in buying or selling, it usually causes a ripple effect in most or all of the remaining exchanges. There are Stock Exchanges located in many parts of the word including Africa, South America, Canada (Toronto), the U. S. (both NYC and Philadelphia), Australia, India (Bombay), China (Hong Kong, Shanghai, Shenzhen), Japan (Tokyo), Europe (Frankfurt, Germany; London, England; Madrid, Spain; Milan, Italy; Moscow, Russia; Switzerland and Norway).

Significance

The Stock Exchanges began as mutual organizations owned by the stock brokers who were their members. In the 21st century the trend of members selling their shares in IPOs or Initial Public Offerings began. These sales have moved stock exchanges from mutual organizations to the status of corporations with shares listed on their own stock exchanges. An example of this would be the Euronext Exchange and the New York Exchange which merged together in 2005 as two corporations. The AMEX Exchange in Philadelphia and the London Exchange followed this pattern and began merger proceedings shortly after.

Fundamentals of the Stock Market

The stock market provides great risk and great rewards.

In spite of the financial risks, investors turn to the stock market because of the possible rewards. According to the Wharton School, a prestigious business education institution, the stock market returns a generous 6.8 percent per year, on average.

Stocks

When you purchase a stock, you are exchanging money for a small part of the company in question. Each "share" entitles you to a part of the company's financial success. Unfortunately, the owner of a stock will lose money if the company decreases in value.

Different kinds of stocks each provide a different level of control over a company. Preferred and common stock, for example, may or may not offer the voting privileges that allow shareholders to determine a firm's leadership.

Stock Market

The stock market, as the Christian Science Monitor points out, is the combined value of all available stocks. Investors may make several kinds of trades, including buying stocks outright or "shorting" them when he believes the value will decrease.

Returns

Stockholders make money by selling shares when the value is greater than the purchase price. Shareholders can also receive a dividend: a payment per share that is determined by the company's performance in the previous year.

Characteristics of the Stock Market

The stock market in the United States is made up of stock exchanges such as the New York Stock Exchange (NYSE) and NASDAQ and self-regulating organizations such as the Pink Sheets, where smaller companies trade over the counter. The NYSE has acquired the American Stock Exchange, the Pacific Stock Exchange, the Philadelphia Stock Exchange, and others.

Growth Capital

Issuing of stock is the cornerstone of capital formation for enterprise in capitalist economic systems. The stock market provides a way for companies to issue stock to the investing public.

Liquidity

The free and transparent trading that takes place in the stock market prices all stocks according to demand and supply, bid and ask. In this way it provides liquidity for investors seeking to transact sales of their holdings through this active pricing mechanism.

Transparency

The public nature of trading maintains transparency in financial transactions. Efficiency, growth, freedom and variety are all possible because of transparency that allows all participants to access the bid and ask prices of all securities traded on the market and because all participants have access to the same information.

Organization

The stock market provides a degree of protection to investors through oversight by the SEC, FINRA and other legal regulatory and self-regulating bodies on state and professional levels that serve to create an organized and liquid group of stock exchanges and stock trading platforms.

Economic Indicator

One of the ten components of the Leading Economic Indicators is made up of the Standard & Poor's 500 Stock Index, one of the major stock market indexes. The direction of trading activity in the stock market provides an indication of the state of commerce and overall confidence in the economy.

Regulated Risk/Reward

An organized and regulated stock market serves as a way for investors who seek large returns on their investments to access organized, liquid, regulated and transparent risk investing.

How to Find Good Stocks to Invest in Stock Market

Your ability to pick good stocks depends on two factors and these are the research that you put in the stock market as well as how much informed you are about the stock market as well as the overall economy.

The definition of good stocks can vary however the stocks that have solid earnings and are leaders in their categories are definitely good stocks. These good stocks should have strong fundamentals. So invest your time wisely in doing fundamental analysis of each stock.

(1) Look for stocks which have strong record of earnings and that will give you confidence that the company's management is good and the stock's EPS is rising every year. This also indicates that the company will be able to service the equity.

(2) The P/E ratio of the company should be comparable to other companies in the

market. This tells a lot about the stock compared to the others in the industry.

(3) The Debt equity ratio of the company should be low which indicates that the company knows how to manage cash and also has good cash flows for investing in expanding the market as well as acquiring good companies.

(4) If you are a dividend investor then look at the dividend payout of the company and a good company will always have the good history of payout even in challenging times.

(5) Look at industry in which the stock is in operation. For example if you invest in the stock of a company which is in conventional cameras then this company will not be doing good in future as the market is currently turning to digital cameras. So invest in companies which are in the emerging markets like nanotechnology.

(6) Look at the overall economy and you should invest in companies that withstand the downturn in the economy. This tells that the company is strong even during the recession.

Notes:

1. **New York Stock Exchange(纽约证券交易所)**: The New York Stock Exchange (NYSE) is a stock exchange located at 11 Wall Street in lower Manhattan, New York City, USA. It is the world's largest stock exchange by market capitalization of its listed companies at U.S. $13.39 trillion as of Dec 2010. Average daily trading value was approximately U.S. $153 billion in 2008. The NYSE is operated by NYSE Euronext, which was formed by the NYSE's 2007 merger with the fully electronic stock exchange Euronext. The NYSE trading floor is located at 11 Wall Street and is composed of four rooms used for the facilitation of trading. A fifth trading room, located at 30 Broad Street, was closed in February 2007. The main building, located at 18 Broad Street, between the corners of Wall Street and Exchange Place, was designated a National Historic Landmark in 1978, as was the 11 Wall Street building.

2. **NASDAQ(National Association of Securities Dealers Automated Quotation)(美国全国证券交易商协会自动报价表)**: The NASDAQ Stock Market, also known as the NASDAQ, is an American stock exchange. It is the largest electronic screen-based equity securities trading market in the United States and second-largest by market capitalization

in the world. As of January 13, 2011, there are 2,872 listings. The NASDAQ has more trading volume than any other electronic stock exchange in the world.

3. **Debt-to-equity ratio**（负债与股东权益比率）: The debt-to-equity ratio (D/E) is a financial ratio indicating the relative proportion of shareholders' equity and debt used to finance a company's assets. Closely related to leveraging, the ratio is also known as Risk, Gearing or Leverage. The two components are often taken from the firm's balance sheet or statement of financial position (so-called book value), but the ratio may also be calculated using market values for both, if the company's debt and equity are publicly traded, or using a combination of book value for debt and market value for equity financially.

4. **IPO**（首次公开募股）: Initial public offering (IPO) is a type of public offering in which shares of a company usually are sold to institutional investors that in turn, sell to the general public, on a securities exchange, for the first time. Through this process, a privately held company transforms into a public company.

5. **EPS**（每股公开收益）: Earnings per share is the monetary value of earnings per outstanding share of common stock for a company.

Words & Expressions:

1. facility [fə'siliti] n. 设施；设备；容易；灵巧
2. shareholder ['ʃeə,həuldə] n. 股东；股票持有人
3. takeover ['teik,əuvə] n. 收购，接管；验收
4. barometer [bə'rɔmitə] n. [气象]气压计；晴雨表；显示变化的事物
5. dividend ['dividend] n. 股息；[数]被除数；奖金
6. prestigious [pre'stidʒəs] adj. 有名望的；享有声望的
7. entitle [in'taitl] vt. 称做……；定名为……；给……称号；使……有权利

8. privilege ['privilidʒ] n. 特权；优待；基本权利
   vt. 给予……特权；特免
9. outright ['autrait] adv. 全部地；立刻地；率直地；一直向前；痛快地
   adj. 完全的，彻底的；直率的；总共的
10. cornerstone ['kɔːnə,stəun] n. 基础；柱石；地基
11. transparency [træns'pærənsi] n. 透明，透明度；幻灯片；有图案的玻璃
12. payout ['pei,aut] n. 支出；花费
13. nanotechnology ['nænəutek'nɔlədʒi] n. 纳米技术
14. withstand [wið'stænd] vt. 抵挡；禁得起；反抗
    vi. 反抗
15. downturn ['dauntəːn] n. 衰退（经济方面）；低迷时期

Exercises:

I. Match the words on the left with their meanings on the right.

1. stockbroker — A. (Initial Public Offerings) a corporation's first offer to sell stock to the public
2. merger agreement — B. (price/earning ratio) the price of a stock divided by its earnings
3. IPO — C. a stock broker's business; charges a fee to act as intermediary between buyer and seller
4. P/E ratio — D. an agent in the buying and selling of stocks and bonds
5. brokerage firm — E. contract governing the merger of two or more companies
6. barometer — F. an instrument that measures atmospheric pressure

II. Fill in the blanks with the suitable words or expressions given in the box. Change the form when necessary.

| payout | dividend | withstand | take over | prestigious |

1. Compelling evidence certainly indicates that human beings are sometimes able to

_____ several hours without oxygen.

2. Was Britain prepared to sacrifice some of its global influence and _____, those choices would be easier.

3. _____ swaps allow investors to separate the income from the capital return of equities.

4. The teenager, who uses a wheelchair, needs round-the-clock care which will be funded by the _____.

5. Undervalued share price can lead to dealership competition and hostile _____.

Ⅲ. Read the following text and fill in the blanks with the words given in the box.

| decentralized | among | vulnerable | buy | traditional | last |

The U. S. Securities and Exchange Commission spent the (1) _____ 15 years trying to encourage more competition (2) _____ stock exchanges. It succeeded. Trading that used to be concentrated on the New York Stock Exchange and NASDAQ today takes place on 11 exchanges. While this (3) _____ approach has lowered costs for investors, it virtually eliminated the (4) _____ market makers who were obliged to (5) _____ and sell stocks when no one else would. Now the SEC is concerned the revolution went too far, leaving markets (6) _____ when selling starts to snowball.

Supplementary Reading

American Stock Markets
—Reversal of Fortune

Numerous threats to the integrity of American public stockmarkets have emerged over the past year, including last May's "flash crash" and—if you believe its critics—NASDAQ's proposal to merge with the New York Stock Exchange. Now another menace is flashing on regulators' radar screens: the "reverse merger", in which a private company goes public by combining with a listed shell company rather than via an initial public offering (IPO).

The practice, also known as "back-door registration", is not new. It has long been used by small firms looking for a cheaper, easier route to public ownership. There are no underwriting fees, for instance. Unfortunately, it also risks allowing dodgy outfits to access public markets, and thus lure investors,  because it enables them to avoid some of the disclosure—and the vetting by regulators, investors and underwriters—to which firms doing IPOs are subject.

The Chinese firms that account for a quarter of the more than 600 back-door registrations since January 2007 are a particular worry. This week Luis Aguilar, one of the five members of the Securities and Exchange Commission (SEC), suggested that a growing number of these have "significant accounting deficiencies" or are "vessels of outright fraud".

At least one back-door registrant has admitted to inventing manufacturing contracts. Another stands accused of staging fake production of biodiesel when investors visited its plant. Several have had to restate earnings.

The focus of most attention, however, is China MediaExpress (CME), an advertising company that reverse-merged its way onto NASDAQ in 2009. Its auditor, Deloitte, resigned last month, citing lost confidence in the firm's financial reporting. This forced CME to reveal that Deloitte had had concerns on many fronts: the authenticity of bank statements, the validity of advertising agents and customers, undisclosed loans and double-counting of the buses on which the firm was supposed to run ads. One of CME's big shareholders is Starr International, run by AIG's former boss, Hank Greenberg. It has sued CME and Deloitte to recover its $13.5 million investment.

Eager to stamp out any shenanigans, the SEC has set up a group to investigate fraud in foreign companies with American listings. But scarred investors should not hold their breath. The firms they backed may be registered in America but many of the documents relating to alleged misconduct, and the people behind them, are beyond the reach of authorities.

Some of their beancounters are out of reach, too. A recent report by America's Public Company Accounting Oversight Board (PCAOB) found that some American audit firms had signed off on the accounts of reverse-merged firms even though their opinion was based largely on work done by unrelated Chinese auditors, in breach of PCAOB guidelines. American regulators are blocked from inspecting audit firms in China. James Doty, the PCAOB's chairman, has called this "a gaping hole in investor protection".

Legitimate operators—yes, they exist—complain that all Chinese "small-cap" shares are being tarred with the same brush. Some are contemplating going private. As they weigh their options, pressure will grow on regulators to scrap the reverse-merger structure. Exchanges that list reverse mergers, such as NASDAQ and NYSE Amex, have delisted or halted trading in at least a dozen stocks (some of which still trade in over-the-counter markets). NASDAQ has tightened listing procedures and started using investigative firms to scout applicants' domestic operations. By one estimate the combined market value of reverse-merged firms peaked at $50 billion. It is unlikely to be surpassed.

Tips

常用股市词汇：
share, equity, stock   股票、股权
bond, debenture, debts   债券
market capitalization   市值
bonus share   红股
dividend   红利/股息
merger and acquisition   收购兼并
capital market   资本市场
monetary market   货币市场
blue chips   蓝筹股
red chips   红筹股
open/close a position   建/平仓

Unit 2

International Marketing

Text A Business Planning—Marketing Planning

> 导读：市场营销策划，首先，应当做前期市场调研；其次，制定营销组合策略，"产品（Product）、价格（Price）、渠道（Place）、促销（Promotion）"四大营销组合策略被概括成"4P"；最后，要确定市场营销工具。

Step 1: Market Research

An essential part of the business planning process is market research. This may include:

Looking at the market—how big is the market? What type of consumers are we aiming to attract? What is the spending pattern of the target consumers? Are there any other market segments we could adapt the product to meet? For example, putting orange juice into mini-cartons to tap into the packed lunch market.

Looking at the product—this may mean some test marketing on a focus group or representative group of consumers and seeing what their reaction is.

Competitors—who are the key competitors? How can we differentiate our product from theirs? Where are they located? How have their sales been changing recently? What prices do they charge? Where do they sell their products or services?

Price—we may need to test how sensitive consumers are to price changes (how elastic is the price?).

Distribution—what are the most appropriate shops or outlets to sell the product in? What are their price expectations?

Promotions—if you are proposing any promotions or other advertising then it may be worth research to see what the reaction of consumers will be to these promotions.

Types of market research—There are two main types of market research. These are desk research (or secondary research) and field research (primary research).

Desk research is research using secondary data. This is data that has already been found by someone and published. This may mean:

Using government published statistics—perhaps from the Office for National Statistics or from international organizations.

Using existing market research information from specialist market research companies.

Using sales figures from competitors (if they can be acquired), together with pricing and product information, perhaps from their promotional information.

Trade associations—many trade associations gather data from all firms in a particular sector and publish the data.

Internet—many web sites offer information and much government published data can be accessed for free through their web sites.

Field research is research that collects primary data. This is data or information that does not already exist. It can be collected through:

Customer questionnaires

Focus group

Direct mail surveys

Web-based surveys

Customer interviews

....

However, results do have to be treated with caution where the sample cannot be controlled, as the sample may not be representative of the population you are trying to reach.

Step 2: Marketing Mix

Another vital part of building a business plan is to determine the marketing mix that you are planning to use. The marketing mix is the balance of marketing techniques required for selling the product. Your marketing mix is a combination of marketing tools that are used to satisfy customers and company objectives. Its components are often known as the four Ps:

Price—the price of the product-particularly the price compared to your competitors a vital part of marketing. There are two possible pricing techniques:

Market skimming—pricing high but selling fewer.

Market penetration—pricing lower to secure a higher volume of sales.

Product—targeting the market and making the product appropriate to the market segment you are trying to sell into.

Promotion—this may take the form of point of sale promotion, advertising, sponsorship or other promotions.

Place—this part of the marketing mix is all about how the product is distributed. Current trends are towards shortening the chain of distribution.

There are those that now refer to another 3Ps bringing the total to 7! The other three are people, physical environment and process.

People—this stresses the importance of people in the marketing process; often the first point of contact with any business is a human being—the impressions given by this initial contact may be very important. In addition, the role of human beings in developing customer relations is seen as increasingly important especially in a knowledge driven economy.

Physical environment—this refers to the importance in making the physical environment related to the product or service as welcoming and as reflective of the business as possible—for example, look at the showrooms of car dealers—many are very well lit, stylish in terms of furniture and decoration and include seating areas, coffee making facilities, newspapers and children's play areas.

Process—the process by which the product is either manufactured or passed on to the final user. This might include the extended use of ICT facilities to speed up ordering, delivery, etc.

The business plan will need details of all of these. What will your price be and why? How will you distribute the goods or service? How will you promote the product? What is the unique selling point (USP) of your product? All these questions need to be answered in the business plan.

Step 3: Marketing Tools

To help you develop your marketing plan, you need to think which marketing tools are likely to be appropriate to your business. The promotion of the business will be the key to building sales and so this is a vital area to consider.

There are two main types of promotion and these are:

Above the line promotion—above the line promotion is promotion that is carried out through independent media that enable a firm to reach a wide audience easily. These might include newspapers and television.

Below the line promotion—below the line promotion is promotion over which the firm has direct control. It includes methods of direct promotion like direct mailing, exhibitions and trade fairs and sales promotions.

The choice of promotional techniques is unlikely to be heavily dependent on the sort of marketing budget that is available, and a business start-up is unlikely to look as much at above the line promotion in its early days.

Choosing the appropriate medium for your promotion is important. The firm will want the maximum exposure to the most appropriate audience to ensure people are as aware as possible about the product, service or brand. Possible choices might include:

Trade journals—these may be effective if your target market is a specialist one, but the journal needs to be one that is widely distributed. Examples of Trade Journals are Variety-covering film, television and stage industry, Air Transport World-aimed at airline managers and the Dental Digest-aimed at dentists! (For other examples watch "Have I Got News for You"!)

Newspapers and magazines—once again, you need to consider the target market very carefully. What age groups or socio-economic groups tend to read each of the possible newspapers and magazines? Are they one of your key market segments? Would a company advertising ride on mowers suitable for use in very large gardens be likely to advertise in the *Daily Star*?

Cinema—the potential is there for a good impact with this type of promotion (smaller local adverts have now become common in cinemas), but are you hitting too broad an audience and is this form of advertising therefore cost-effective?

Radio—there are now much larger numbers of local independent radio stations, but again you will need to look carefully that the station matches your target audience, and is it a cost-effective method?

Direct mail—an increasingly common method of promotion. Can you identify your target market easily and perhaps buy a database of suitable names and addresses?

Television—this can be an effective advertising medium, but is likely to be closed off to most business start-ups on grounds of cost. The average price for a 30 seconds ad in prime time TV can be around £80,000 rising to £120,000 during peak time viewing.

Sales promotions / discount schemes—you could offer start-up discounts or vouchers that are delivered to people. Other possibilities might include competitions, product endorsements, free offers or perhaps special sales / credit terms.

Exhibitions/trade fairs—once again, these may be effective if your audience is a fairly specialist one and the exhibition targets them effectively. The Motor Show, The Boat Show, The Ideal Homes Exhibition and the Chelsea Flower Show are all examples of exhibitions where relevant businesses might be keen to expose their products and services.

Point of sale promotion—could you encourage outlets to have promotional materials to help with promotion where the product is sold? Look at the items available at the counter of your local supermarket, petrol station and newsagent!

Personal selling—this method is most likely to be appropriate where the product is likely to be sold in large numbers to a small number of clients and would involve employing a sales representative.

The choice of which medium you use is likely to be down to a number of factors, and these might include:

Cost

How well the method reaches the target market

The behavior of competitors

Legal restrictions

How well the medium enables you to reach your desired marketing mix

The effectiveness of the medium and the impact it has

Notes:

1. **Air Transport World（ATW）(世界航空运输):** a monthly trade magazine covering the airline industry. They also provide an online version (www.atwonline.com) with daily air transport news. The publication covers airline operations, market conditions, management, and related issues. Each year, it publishes a World Airline Report covering the state of the industry, and selects an Airline of the Year on the basis of operational excellence.

2. *Daily Star* (《每日之星》): a newspaper published in Oneonta, New York, United States.

3. **The RHS Chelsea Flower Show（切尔西花展）:** officially the Great Spring Show, is a garden show held each year for five days in May by the Royal Horticultural Society (RHS) in the grounds of the Royal Hospital Chelsea in Chelsea, London. It is the most famous such show in the United Kingdom, perhaps the most famous gardening event in the world and part of London's summer social season. Popular parts of the Chelsea Flower Show include the show gardens designed by leading names and the centrepiece of the floral marquee.

Words & Expressions:

1. segment ['segmənt] n. 段；部分
2. tap into 挖掘；接近
3. elastic [i'læstik] adj. 有弹性的；灵活的；易伸缩的
    n. 松紧带；橡皮圈
4. outlet ['autlet] n. 销售点；批发商点
5. component [kəm'pəunənt] n. 成分；组件；元件
6. distribution [,distri'bju:ʃən] n. 分布；分配
7. penetration [,peni'treiʃən] n. 渗透；突破；侵入；洞察力
8. sponsorship ['spɔnsəʃip] n. 赞助
9. showroom ['ʃəuru:m] n. 陈列室；样品间
10. stylish ['stailiʃ] adj. 时髦的；现代风格的；潇洒的
11. trade journal 行业杂志，行业刊物
12. socio-economic [,səusi'-i:kə'nɔmik] adj. 社会经济的
13. mower ['məuə] n. 割草机；割草的人
14. advert [əd'və:t] vi. 注意；谈到 n. 广告
15. direct mail 直接邮件；直接邮寄广告
16. on grounds of 以……为理由；根据……
17. voucher ['vautʃə] n. 收据；证人；保证人；证明者
18. endorsement [in'dɔ:smənt] n. 认可；背书；签注（文件）
19. discount ['diskaunt] n. 折扣
    v. 贴现；打折扣出售商品
20. special sales 特价销售

Exercises:

I. Fill in the blanks with the suitable words or expressions given in the box. Change the form when necessary.

sponsor	volume	on grounds of	tap into	outlet

1. To understand the American slang you really have to _____ the whole culture.

2. Food and beverage _____ are available within the exhibition area for exhibitors and visitors.

3. Large _____ of data were gathered because of the research.

4. More and more Chinese athletes are taking commercial _____ but they have to share the rewards with the government.

5. The Board agreed to Johnson's retirement _____ ill health.

II. Translate the following phrases into Chinese or English.

1. desk research
2. field research
3. sales figures
4. sale promotion
5. car dealer
6. 赞助商
7. 独家卖点
8. 行业杂志
9. 直接邮寄
10. 特价销售

III. Read the following text and fill in the blanks with the words given in the box.

| recognized | rising | account | enterprises | registrations |
| trademarks | percent | branch | accordance | statistics |

Beijing has seen robust growth in trademark (1) _____ in recent years, but there is still a long way to go for the city to own more globally (2) _____ trademarks, authorities said on Monday.

The city holds more than 250,000 (3) _____ and the number is (4) _____ every year, according to the Beijing Administration for Industry and Commerce (BAIC).

In Chaoyang district alone, from 2006 to 2009, trademark registrations grew by 24.7 (5) _____ each year.

So far, the district owns about 60,000 trademarks, of which business services, finance and modern service industries (6) _____ for 36 percent, according to (7) _____ released by BAIC's Chaoyang (8) _____ at the Summit on Implementing Trademark Strategy and Promoting Brand Development that took place on Monday.

The increasing number of trademark registrations is in (9) _____ with the growing awareness of trademark protection among (10) _____.

Text B Supporting Offline Campaign Launches with Online Marketing

> 导读：网上营销也称为网络营销，就是以国际互联网络为基础，利用数字化的信息和网络媒体的交互性来辅助营销目标实现的一种新型的市场营销方式。简单地说，网络营销就是以互联网为主要手段，为达到一定营销目的而进行的营销活动。

As the U. S. online audience begins to see the last of the unconnected users begin serious uptake, and many formerly light and medium users move to a persistent connection, a full integration of Internet marketing into all marketing becomes increasingly critical.

There is more to integrated marketing than just repeating the same message in different channels. And, it is not an easy task to get the right balance of in-store promotions, mass advertising and online marketing in one campaign. So how should a brand manager use the online channel as part of the marketing mix when launching a new product?

Based on our experience with consumer goods companies, we have found that there are a few key guidelines that must be kept closely in mind when attempting to use the Internet channel to launch new products.

(1) Web sites should be an extension of product packaging. Since your product packaging has limited space for everything you would like to communicate, you should use your web site as an opportunity for consumers to learn more about your product. Consumers expect to find useful product information on your site, such as recipes, nutrition information, tips and tools on usage, store location and contact information. Most consumers are not interested in viewing commercials and advertising as they are not using their monitors as TV screens. Slim-fast is a good example of a site providing relevant content to its target audience, such a recipes, diet plans, weight control tools and exercise advice.

The challenge in effectively making your site an extension of packaging is finding innovative ways to drive consumers to your web site. Campbell Soup Company, for instance, found a way of engaging the consumers with the Chunky brand while  entertaining them at the same time. Chunky printed a football trivia question on each can, driving consumers to visit their site for the answer, and then could continue playing the trivia game by choosing different varieties and questions. Driving consumers to the web site provided the opportunity not only to promote all soup varieties, but also to communicate the launch of the new chili products.

(2) Web sites should be "lifestyle" destinations. With today's increased Internet use, this is an effective strategy. A "lifestyle" site focuses on providing appealing content beyond the traditional brand-related information. The key however is to develop a plan for ongoing maintenance, giving the consumers a good reason to come back and engage with the brand over time.

SoBe Juices and Jones Soda are two companies that have done an excellent job in creating true "lifestyle" sites? They are both effectively targeting teens with engaging content. Their sites feature stories, events and downloadable content that are refreshed on a regular basis keeping the sites interesting and continually engaging visitors.

This strategy involves a long-term commitment, which could be difficult for one brand to sustain on its own. As a brand manager, you should consider partnering with other brands within your company that target the same demographic. A good example of this strategy is Procter and Gamble's teen girls' web site. Another way to sustain this strategy is to partner with a "lifestyle" publisher of content to provide the audience with fresh updates in a magazine-style manner, such as iVillage.

(3) Promotions engage customers. If your target audience is heavy online media users you should consider creating an online promotion, such as a sweepstakes to break through a crowded market when launching a new product. The promotional site is especially tailored to a promotion with a clear path of actions that the consumer should take. A promotional site is different from a company's corporate site, which can distract the user with links to areas non-related to your campaign. At the point of registration, you could also seize the opportunity to include product related survey questions. Encouraging users to register will help you build a comprehensive consumer database for future direct marketing activities.

(4) 2-way communication is essential. In fact, you should solicit feedback and make the consumer feel like "part of the family" instead of solely focusing on the sell. This is an excellent opportunity to learn about how your target audience perceives the product and learn how it fits into their lives. It could give you great insight on potential product improvements or extensions.

(5) Encourage trial with online coupons. When launching a new product, using online coupons as a purchase incentive has been very effective for many CPG companies. Consumers are turning to the Internet as a source for coupons, redeemable both online and off-line. The top web sites for coupons are currently CoolSavings and ValuPage.

(6) Encourage word-of-Mouth. You should provide your site visitors the ability to forward links to their friends either via email or instant messaging. When a product offering is compelling, you'd be surprised how many people will forward to their friends.

(7) Plan for channel-appropriate and holistic measurement. It is largely beyond debate that exposing the consumer to your message through a variety of media has a greater impact on your bottom line. Likewise, a successful multi-channel marketing effort uses the best practices of multiple channels, in this case both classic segmentation and media mix, across traditional and Internet channels. The key is to identify all touch points and how the content should differ between the channels and make sure you include a measurement strategy inclusive of each.

If your web site goal is to have every site visitor register for the newsletter, then measure this conversion. If you are launching a new product on the market and your goal is to measure purchase intent, then your success metric should not be based on banner click-through, instead it should be measured on the branding impact. The key is to set realistic measurement goals up front, and make provisions for accurate and applicable measurement afterwards.

Notes:

1. **Campbell Soup Company**（金宝汤公司）：(NYSE: CPB), also known as Campbell's, is a well-known American producer of canned soups and related products. Campbell's products are sold in 120 countries around the world. It is headquartered in Camden, New Jersey. Campbell's divides itself into three divisions: the Simple Meals division which consists largely of Soups both condensed and ready to serve, the Baked Snacks division that consists of Pepperidge Farm, and the Health Beverage Division that includes V8 juices. The company has undertaken a major initiative since 2008 to reduce the sodium content of its products, especially canned soups.

2. **iVillage, Inc.**（女性媒体公司）：a media company that is owned by NBC Universal. The site focuses on categories targeted at women, including Food, Health, Entertainment, Family, Beauty & Style. Additional businesses and brand extensions within iVillage Networks include iVillage UK, NBC Digital Health Network, Astrology.com and GardenWeb. In addition, iVillage has a strategic partnership with BlogHer, a participatory news, entertainment and information network for women online. iVillage has approximately 34 million unique visitors per month (comScore, April 2010), making it the largest content-driven community for women on the web.

Words & Expressions:

1. uptake [ˈʌpteik] n. 摄取；领会；举起
2. persistent [pəˈsistənt] adj. 固执的，坚持的；持久稳固的
3. integration [ˌintiˈgreiʃən] n. 集成；综合

4. offline ['ɔflain] n. 脱机；挂线
   adj. 脱机的；离线的，未连线的
5. forthcoming ['fɔ:θ'kʌmiŋ] adj. 即将来临的
6. quantification [,kwɔntifi'keiʃən] n. 定量，量化
7. recipe ['resipi] n. 食谱；[医]处方；秘诀
8. trivia ['triviə] n. 琐事
9. chili ['tʃili] n. 红辣椒，辣椒
10. teen [ti:n] n. 青少年（等于 teenager）
11. demographic [,demə'græfik] adj. 人口统计学的；人口学的
12. sweepstakes ['swi:psteiks] n. 赌金；比赛
13. tailor ['teilə] vt. 剪裁；使合适
    n. 裁缝
    vi. 做裁缝
14. distract [dis'trækt] vt. 转移；分心
15. solicit [sə'lisit] vt. & vi. 征求；招揽；请求；乞求
16. feedback ['fi:dbæk] n. 反馈；成果，资料；回复
17. coupon ['ku:pɔn] n. 息票；赠券；联票；配给券
18. incentive [in'sentiv] n. 动机；刺激
    adj. 激励的；刺激的
19. redeemable [ri'di:məbl] adj. 可赎回的；可偿还的；可挽救的；可换成现款的
20. compelling [kəm'peliŋ] adj. 引人注目的；强制的；激发兴趣的
21. holistic [həu'listik] adj. 整体的；全盘的
22. segmentation [,segmən'teiʃən] n. 分割；割断；细胞分裂

Exercises:

I. **Translate the following phrases into Chinese or English.**

1. light and medium users

2. in-store promotions
3. mass advertising
4. brand manager
5. feature story
6. 营销手法
7. 营销组合
8. 线下和网上营销活动
9. 推出新产品
10. 产品包装

II. Decide whether the following statements are true (T) or false (F) according to the passage.

1. There is less to integrated marketing than just repeating the same message in different channels. (   )
2. Web sites should be an extension of product packaging. (   )
3. The challenge in effectively making your site an extension of packaging is finding innovative ways to drive consumers to your web site. (   )
4. If your target audience is heavy online media users you should consider creating an offline promotion, such as a sweepstakes to break through a crowded market when launching a new product. (   )
5. When launching a new product, using online coupons as a purchase incentive has been very effective for many CPG companies. (   )

III. Read the following text and fill in the blanks with the words given in the box.

| emotion | strategies | consumers | distribution | resources |
| decision | focusing | operate | benefits | effective |

When you are marketing to a B2B you want to focus on the logic of the product. You do this by (1) _____ on the features of the product. There is little to no personal (2) _____ involved in the purchasing (3) _____. You want to focus on understanding the organizational buyers and how they (4) _____ within the confines of their organization's procedures. The B2B market has a thirst for knowledge and they are information seekers. Be more in-depth with your marketing materials. Your most (5) _____ marketing message will focus on how your product or service saves them time, money and (6) _____.

When you are marketing to a consumer you want to focus on the (7) _____ of the product. Their decision is more emotional. (8) _____ are different in that they demand a variety of (9) _____ channels for convenience, not so with the B2B market. Consumers are less likely to be interested in a lengthy marketing message. They will want you to get right to the point. Consumers don't want to work to understand your benefits; instead they will want you to clearly point out the benefits to them. Your most effective marketing (10) _____ will focus on the results and the benefits that your product or service will bring to them.

Supplementary Reading

Online-coupon Firms —Groupon Anxiety

Groupon has arrived in China. On March 16th the online-coupon firm's new site there—a joint venture with Tencent, the country's biggest Internet company—began offering daily deals such as 75% off the regular price of a trip to an indoor hot-springs resort.

Initial signs were that Chinese consumers will rush to snap up Groupon's offers, as they have in many other parts of the world.

In 2009 Groupon was a virtual nobody, confined to just 30 American cities, with 120 employees, 2m subscribers and just $33m in revenues. By the end of 2010 it had become a global success, with more than 4,000 staff, 51m subscribers in 565 cities worldwide and $760m in revenues.

Yet amid all the excitement over the "world's fastest-growing company ever", as some have breathlessly described Groupon, words of caution can increasingly be heard. Even Andrew Mason, the firm's habitually cheerful boss, seems to harbour doubts. "By this time next year, we will either be on our way to becoming one of the great technology brands", he recently wrote in an internal memo, "or a cool idea by people who were out-executed and out-innovated by others." More fundamentally, the whole idea of "daily deals" may have serious flaws.

The basic idea is nothing new. Consumers sign up to receive offers from local firms by E-mail each day, ranging from restaurant meals to pole-dancing lessons, at discounts of up to 90%. But Groupon made virtual coupon-clipping exciting by, first, having offers expire after just a few hours and, second, cancelling them if they do not attract a minimum number of buyers (the "group" in Groupon). Although this rarely happens, it induces buyers to spread the word among friends and family, boosting the uptake.

The daily frenzy has already spawned new phrases, such as "Groupon anxiety" — "the preoccupation and feeling of anxiousness and not being able to sleep knowing that a new Groupon will be released after 1am", according to The Urban Dictionary, a website which tracks such coinages.

Unlike lightly staffed but equally hyped Internet firms such as Facebook and Twitter, Groupon needs an army of salespeople to negotiate deals with local businesses in each city it covers, and a further platoon of bright young copywriters to churn out the witty, whimsical E-mail pitches it sends out to consumers.

What makes Groupon really stand out, however, are its margins. It typically charges businesses half of the discounted price of a voucher. Venture capitalists say they have never seen such impressive numbers. This goes a long way towards explaining why the start-up was able to raise a whopping $1.1 billion in financing and why, in December, Google was willing to pay an even more astounding $6 billion for it.

Mr Mason walked away from the deal and has started the process of getting a public listing. This decision may come to haunt him. Groupon's position is not as unassailable as it appears from its rapid growth and huge market share—more than 60% in America, according to neXtup Research, which analyses tech firms. To ward off competition, neXtup reckons, Groupon will be forced to lower the share of revenue it keeps from its deals.

Deals a dime a dozen

For starters, almost anyone can set up a daily-deals site. And many already have. There are hundreds of clones in America alone, most specializing in certain product categories. To help overwhelmed consumers, there is even a service, The Dealmap, which lists all the daily deals available in a city. More dangerously for Groupon, big online firms have begun to enter the fray. In December Amazon invested $175m in LivingSocial, the market's number two, which is said to be in talks to raise a further $500m. And Facebook, the world's biggest social network, will soon start testing local discounts.

In addition, Groupon cannot rely on the "network effects"

that have given companies such as Facebook and eBay, the world's biggest online-auction site, an almost unassailable lead: the more users such services have, the more valuable they become, thus attracting even more users. In the case of Groupon the network effects are comparatively weak. Being the biggest kid on the block is certainly an advantage: a long mailing list attracts better merchants, which pull in more consumers. But both businesses and consumers can easily switch to other sites.

Groupon's managers are aware of all this. Rob Solomon, its chief operating officer, agrees that the barriers to entering the daily-deals market are low and the network effects weak. However, he believes that, with the right strategy, the company can create competitive barriers to shore up its dominant position. One way it is doing so is to make better use of all the data it collects, for instance to personalize deals and help local businesses design their Groupon offers. Last year the firm hired as chief data officer an executive from Netflix, a film-rental business noted for its data-mining skills. In America Groupon already tailors some offers depending on the sex, location and buying history of a subscriber.

The next step is for Groupon to become a broader "platform for local commerce", in the words of Mr. Solomon—a bundle of services that make that market more efficient. In America it has already started testing virtual storefronts where a city's businesses can organize their own deals. It is said to be working on a smartphone application that alerts consumers to a local business's special offers whenever they walk past its real-life storefront.

Besides having to keep one step ahead of its many competitors, there is another reason why Groupon needs to grow into a broader local-commerce operation: the daily-deals phenomenon, despite its remarkable recent growth, may have its limits. Although Mr. Solomon claims that 95% of local firms using Groupon come back for more, independent research comes up with markedly less impressive numbers. Last summer Utpal Dholakia of Rice University interviewed 150 businesses that had done Groupon promotions. One-third said they did not make any money from them, and 42% said that they would not do another daily deal.

The reasons for such numbers are various. Businesses grumble that the deals attract mainly bargain-hunters who do not spend more than the coupon's face value and do not become repeat customers. Although these problems may be fixed by designing the promotions better, there are some longer-term worries. Studies have repeatedly shown that price discounts erode brand value, says Mr. Dholakia. They may be good for giving businesses some exposure but the benefit of this is likely to wear off after a few such promotions. Mr. Solomon will have none of this, calling Mr. Dholakia's survey unrepresentative and insisting that Groupon has a queue of new companies keen to sign up.

Even so, there is a risk that local businesses, having given Groupon a try, will abandon it. How the behaviour of consumers will evolve is harder to predict. So far the hunger for online coupons seems insatiable. Groupon's best customers are young, female city-dwellers, who tend to be avid followers of fashion; but fashions change. Mr. Dholakia has already seen signs of what the Urban Dictionary will probably call "Groupon fatigue".

Does this mean that Groupon will go the way of Napster, Friendster or MySpace, all of which had meteoric rises before crashing and burning? This is clearly a risk. But with its powerful momentum, strong management and hefty financial backing, the firm certainly has a chance of becoming the dominant platform for local service businesses to pull in the punters, much as Amazon has come to dominate online shopping for all sorts of physical goods. If so, though, daily deals will probably be just one of Groupon's offerings.

Tips

常用市场营销促销词汇：

bargain sale　大减价
clearance sale　清仓大甩卖
jumble sale　旧货廉卖
rebate　部分退款；贴现
free gift　赠品
free trial　免费试用
distress price　跳楼价
coupons　优惠券
show window　旺铺橱窗
tie-in sale　搭售

Unit 3

Business Elite

Text A The Resurrection of Steve Jobs

—That Which Does Not Kill the Boss of Apple Seems to Make Him Stronger

> 导读：商务精英史蒂夫·保罗·乔布斯已俨然成为电子商务史上的一个奇迹。他惊人的电脑天赋、平易近人的处世风格、绝妙的创意脑筋、处变不惊的领导风范筑就了苹果企业文化的核心内容，苹果公司的雇员对他的崇敬简直就是一种宗教般的狂热。雇员甚至自豪地对外面的人说："我为乔布斯工作！"

One morning, about a year ago (2004), a doctor told Steve Jobs that a cancerous tumour in his pancreas would kill him within months, and that it was time to start saying his goodbyes. Later that night, an endoscopy revealed that the tumour could be cut out. But for one day Mr. Jobs, the boss of Apple Computer, as well as Pixar, the world's most successful animation studio, stared death in the face.

The experience seems to have invigorated him. Last week, gaunter but otherwise undiminished, he was on a stage in San Francisco, putting on a show (for that is what Apple product launches are) that was as flashy and dynamic as any as he has ever thrown. When businessmen try to rub shoulders with pop stars, the effect is usually embarrassing. But "Steve" had arranged to have his pal, Madonna, pop up on screen and kidded around with her with panache. Does she have an iPod? Of course she has! "That's so duh," said the superstar playfully. Then Mr. Jobs segued into his announcements—a new mobile phone from Motorola that has iTunes, Apple's music software, pre-installed and that represents a beachhead into the world of phones; and the "iPod nano", a new digital music-player that is thinner than a pencil, but still holds 1,000 songs.

For Mr. Jobs, the product launch seemed mainly to be an opportunity to drive home the message that his hold on downloaded and portable music now seems overwhelming. iTunes sells 2m songs a day and has a world market share of 82%—Mr. Jobs reckons that it is the world's second-largest Internet store, behind only Amazon. And the iPod has a market share of 74%, with 22m sold. For a man who helped launch the personal-computer era in 1976 with the Apple I, but then had to watch Microsoft's Bill Gates walk away with, in effect, the monopoly on PC operating systems (Apple's market share in computers today is less than 3%), this must be some vindication.

The odd thing about near-death experiences—literal or metaphorical—in Mr. Jobs's life is that he seems actually to need them sporadically in order to thrive. Mr. Jobs himself suggested as much when he addressed the graduating class at Stanford University in June. Until he turned 30 in 1985, Mr. Jobs led a life that fits almost every Silicon Valley cliché. He dropped out of college (like Bill Gates and Michael Dell); he started a company with a friend in a garage (like everybody from Hewlett and Packard to the founders of Google); he launched a revolution (the PC era). Big deal. The interesting event occurred when he was 30 and got fired from his own company, after Apple's board turned against him. He was "devastated". His career seemed dead.

Characteristically, though, Mr. Jobs bounced back, once he realized, as he said at Stanford, that "the heaviness of being successful was replaced by the lightness of being a beginner again." He did something uninterrupted success might have made impossible: he became more creative. In 1986 he started two new companies, NeXT, a computer-maker that was always too far ahead of its time, and Pixar, an animation studio that went on to have a series of box-office hits. A decade later, ironically enough, NeXT was bought by Apple, and

Mr. Jobs was brought back to run the company he had founded.

Mr. Jobs, a pescatarian (ie, a vegetarian who eats fish) with a philosophical streak and a strong interest in the occult, interprets these reversals as lessons. As befits a man who grew up in California in the 1960s, he proclaims his belief in karma and in love. Not necessarily love of his employees, apparently—some of whom have found working for him a nightmare—but love of one's ideals. Always do only what you love, and never settle, he advised the students at Stanford. His brush with cancer, in particular, seems to have focused his mind. "Death is very likely the single best invention in life," Mr. Jobs told his young audience. "All external expectations, all pride, all fear of embarrassment or failure—these things just fall away in the face of death, leaving only what is truly important."

Do not get the impression that Mr. Jobs is now hugging strangers in random acts of kindness. He is still testy, irascible and difficult; he is still prepared to sue teenagers who publish Apple gossip on their websites for alleged abuses of trade secrets. But the reminders of mortality have changed him. "He was already softened" after his public humbling in 1985, says Bruce Chizen, the boss of Adobe Systems, a software company that is a long-time partner of Apple's. After the cancer, he says, "he's even softer" and, Mr. Chizen reckons, even more creative.

New toys on the way

Mr. Jobs's rivals may feel the same way. The digerati in Silicon Valley, Redmond (Microsoft), Tokyo (Sony), Seoul (Samsung) and other places now simply take it for granted that Mr. Jobs has a top-secret conveyor belt that will keep churning out best-selling wonders like the iPod. What could these toys be? A portable video player is rumoured. A new and cooler sort of television is possible. A user-friendly and elegant mobile-phone handset would be nice, perhaps called something like "iPhone".

Hollywood and music studios are also increasingly frightened. The music studios, which barely took him seriously when he launched iTunes in 2001, are sick of his power and are pressuring him to change his 99-cents-per-song flat rate for music. Slim chance. Disney, a long-time partner of Pixar whom Mr. Jobs broke with when he got tired of its former boss, is now trying to worm its way back into his favour.

In short, Mr. Jobs currently seems vivacious by anybody's standards. There are even rumours that he might run for governor of California (as a Democrat, presumably; Al Gore is on Apple's board). For somebody famous in large part for a spectacular defeat—to Bill Gates and Microsoft—all this must feel like a new lease of life, in every respect.

Notes:

1. **Steven Paul Jobs**（史蒂夫·保罗·乔布斯）: (born February 24, 1955) is an American business magnate and inventor. He is the co-founder and chief executive officer of Apple Inc. Jobs' history in business has contributed much to the symbolic image of the idiosyncratic, individualistic Silicon Valley entrepreneur, emphasizing the importance of design and understanding the crucial role aesthetics play in public appeal. His work driving forward the development of products that are both functional and elegant has earned him a devoted following.

2. **Pixar Animation Studios**（皮克斯动画工作室）: an American CGI animation film studio based in Emeryville, California, United States. Pixar became a subsidiary of The Walt Disney Company in 2006. The studio has earned twenty-six Academy Awards, seven Golden Globes, and three Grammys, among many other awards and acknowledgments. Its films have made over $6.3 billion worldwide.

3. **Michael Dell**（迈克尔·戴尔）: (born February 23, 1965) is an American business magnate and the founder and chief executive officer of Dell Inc. He is one of the richest people in the world, with a net worth of U.S. $14 billion in 2010.

4. **Al Gore**（戈尔）: Albert Arnold "Al" Gore, Jr. (born March 31, 1948) served as the 45th Vice President of the United States (1993—2001), under President Bill Clinton. He was the Democratic Party nominee for President in the 2000 U. S. presidential election. Gore is currently an author, businessman, and environmental activist.

Words & Expressions:

1. pancreas ['pænkriəs] n. [解剖]胰腺
2. endoscopy [en'dɔskəpi] n. [临床]内窥镜检查；内视镜检查法；内视镜室
3. invigorate [in'vigəreit] vt. 鼓舞；使精力充沛
4. gaunt [gɔ:nt] adj. 憔悴的；荒凉的；枯瘦的
5. panache [pə'næʃ] n. 羽饰；灿烂；耍派头
6. beachhead ['bi:tʃhed] n. [军]滩头堡，滩头阵地
7. monopoly [mə'nɔpəli] n. 垄断；垄断者；专卖权
8. sporadically [spə'rædikəli] adv. 零星地；偶发地
9. occult [ə'kʌlt] adj. 神秘的；超自然的；难以理解的
   vt. 掩蔽
   n. 神秘学
   vi. 被掩
10. karma ['kɑ:mə] n. 因果报应，因缘
11. irascible [i'ræsəbl] adj. 易怒的
12. churn out 艰苦地做出；大量炮制
13. vivacious [vi'veiʃəs] adj. 活泼的；快活的；有生气的

Exercises:

Ⅰ. **Fill in the blanks with the suitable words given in the box. Change the form when necessary.**

beachhead	monopoly	vivacious	churn out
gaunt	sporadically	invigorate	irascible

1. It has given me great consolation and delight to see such a _____ younger generation.
2. Yet this is where Tesco, Britain's biggest supermarket group, will seek to establish its _____ in the world's richest grocery market.

3. What's more, any laboratory equipped to make vaccines can easily _____ deadly biological material.

4. They demonstrate that the Ministry of Commerce is serious about implementing its _____ law.

5. He would disappear for months at a time, occasionally showing up _____ and ragged.

6. Their goal was to _____ their economies and international standing by attracting brains, taste and talent.

7. However, diverse political views are aired and the opposition press does function, albeit _____.

8. "What does he come here cheeking us for?" cried Kidderminster, showing _____ temperament.

II. Translate the following sentences into Chinese.

1. For Mr Jobs, the product launch seemed mainly to be an opportunity to drive home the message that his hold on downloaded and portable music now seems overwhelming.

2. The odd thing about near-death experiences—literal or metaphorical—in Mr Jobs's life is that he seems actually to need them sporadically in order to thrive.

3. "Death is very likely the single best invention in life," Mr Jobs told his young audience. "All external expectations, all pride, all fear of embarrassment or failure—these things just fall away in the face of death, leaving only what is truly important."

III. Topic discussion.

1. In your perspective, what kind of person is Steven Paul Jobs? Which personality of his attracts you most?

2. Could you please name out some other business elites around the world who are as distinguished as Mr Jobs?

3. What are the indispensable characteristics a person should possess if he or she trys to become a business elite?

Text B Ann Moore: The CEO of Time

> 导读：30多年来，时代集团总裁安·穆尔女士目睹了杂志业的演变、兴衰。如今，杂志业处境艰难，穆尔女士拟将技术作为解决手段，让科技重振杂志业。她说："这个行业需要使用科学技术，并使之成为我们的优势。"

There are few things that unnerve Ann Moore, the chief executive of Time Inc., America's largest magazine company, as much as young Americans "shock" when they hear that her firm will have to start charging them. "Real reporting takes time and money and effort," she says. "Somebody does have to pay for the Baghdad bureau." A recession is a difficult time to convince readers that they need to start paying for information, however, particularly because Time Inc., a division of Time Warner, a media giant, has long made its articles available free online. But a new model is needed, and Ms. Moore is trying all sorts of things in her effort to find one. On March 18th her company launched Mine, for example, a new concept that allows readers to go online and select articles from eight titles, for delivery in print or online as a free, personalized magazine. If this proves popular, the company may start charging for it. This nifty scheme highlights Time Inc's eagerness to attract readers to its magazines—but its ambivalence about adding a price tag.

As the boss of a company which oversees 120 magazine titles including Time, People, Sports Illustrated and Fortune, Ms. Moore faces the difficult task of keeping magazines relevant as household budgets shrink, the appeal of free content online grows, and advertisers reduce their spending. At some of her magazines, such as Time, advertising revenues are down by around 30% compared with this time last year, according to Media Industry Newsletter. Ms. Moore has had to tear up her company's five-year plan and draft a new two-year one instead, focusing on two things: internal reorganization and innovation.

After laying off around 600 people, Ms. Moore has restructured the firm into three units—news, entertainment and lifestyle—grouping together magazines with similar material, advertisers and audiences. The aim is to maintain editorial quality while increasing efficiency, because titles can share writers and articles and pool resources for functions, such as subscription services. Ms. Moore has also turned her attention to training, launching "Time Inc University", a series of seminars led by Time executives on topics such as branding and teamwork, in February.

Ms Moore will teach one of these seminars herself. Ms. Moore has seen the magazine industry evolve, and weather technological shifts, for over three decades. She graduated from Harvard Business School in 1978 with 13 job offers, including one from Time Inc. She accepted it, even though it paid the least, because she had grown up reading Time and dreamt of working at Sports Illustrated. She started as a financial analyst and rose to become associate publisher of Sports Illustrated, but it soon became clear to her that the magazine, a very male title at a company dominated by men, would not make her publisher in a hurry. So she moved to People in 1991, and helped make it one of the most profitable magazines in the world.

It was at People that Ms Moore was spotted by Richard Parsons, who later became chief executive of Time Warner and chose Ms. Moore as chief executive of Time Inc in 2002. According to Mr. Parsons, who is now chairman of Citigroup, Ms Moore was "bright, charming, energetic, fun and gutsy" and had the skills to "transform Time Inc from a magazine company to a publishing company" that made its output available online as well as in print. But Mr. Parsons, who has watched her career closely, admits that she is now operating in troubled waters, as she tries to cope with a recession in addition to the rise of the Internet.

Ms. Moore is a self-described "magazine optimist" who thinks that holding a glossy magazine beats looking at a screen. Magazines may indeed be better placed than newspapers to cope with the recession and readers' shift towards the web. But given the woes of America's newspapers, many of which have gone bust or shifted to scaled-down, web-only operations, that is not saying much. And despite her love of print, Ms Moore is not afraid of technology. In February Time ran a cover story entitled "How to Save Your Newspaper" which crystallized a growing belief within the industry that providing articles to readers free online is not sustainable, and that a switch to paid access will be necessary. Ms. Moore thinks her firm can lead the way in this shift from freebies to fees. This month Time Inc said it was considering the introduction of a hybrid (or "freemium") scheme, making some People and Time articles available free, but charging for premium content. But this approach has been tried before, notably by the New York Times, which later abandoned it.

Another possibility is that readers may be prepared to subscribe to content on portable devices such as Amazon's Kindle e-reader or advanced "smart" phones. Ms Moore says it might make sense for her company to subsidize such devices if readers agree to sign up for enough material—an approach that would make particular sense for Time Inc., with its wide range of titles. Ms. Moore is already talking to makers of e-readers about working together. The music industry, she notes, missed out because it was afraid to embrace technology. She is determined not to let the same thing happen in magazine publishing.

Notes:

1. **Ann Moore（安·穆尔）**: the Chairman and Chief Executive Officer of Time Inc. She became the company's first female CEO when she was appointed to the position in July 2002.

2. **Time Warner（时代华纳）**: the world's second largest entertainment conglomerate in terms of revenue (behind Disney and ahead of News Corporation and Viacom), as well as the world's largest media conglomerate, headquartered in the Time Warner Center in New York City.

3. **Harvard Business School（HBS）（哈佛商学院）**: the graduate business school of Harvard University in Boston, Massachusetts. The school offers a full-time MBA program, doctoral programs, and many executive education programs.

Unit 3 Business Elite 51

Words & Expressions:

1. unnerve [ʌnˈnəːv] vt. 使失去勇气；使身心交疲；使焦躁；使失常
2. nifty [ˈnifti] adj. 俏皮的；漂亮的
   n. 俏皮话
3. ambivalence [æmˈbivələns] n. 矛盾情绪；正反感情并存
4. shrink [ʃriŋk] vi. 收缩；畏缩
   vt. 使缩小，使收缩
   n. 收缩
5. revenue [ˈrevənjuː] n. 收入；税收；收益；营业收入
6. gutsy [ˈgʌtsi] adj. 勇敢的；贪婪的；有种的；胆大的
7. evolve [iˈvɔlv] vt. 发展，进化；进化；使逐步形成；推断出
   vi. 发展，进展；进化；逐步形成
8. crystallize [ˈkristəˌlaiz] vt. 使结晶；明确；使具体化；做成蜜饯
   vi. 结晶，形成结晶；明确；具体化
9. freeby [ˈfriːbi] n. 免费赠品
10. hybrid [ˈhaibrid] n. 杂种，混血儿；混合物
    adj. 混合的；杂种的
11. premium [ˈpriːmiəm] n. 保险费，额外费用；奖金
12. subsidize [ˈsʌbsidaiz] vt. 资助；给与奖助金；向……行贿

Exercises:

I. Fill in the blanks with the suitable words given in the box. Change the form when necessary.

| shrink | unnerve | ambivalence | evolve | subsidize |
| revenues | nifty | hybrid | available | highlight |

1. He hoped to _____ Kennedy and force him into concessions.

2. Unfortunately, modern protocols and applications have no idea about QOS, so for most LANs, this is just one more very _____ but unused feature.

3. While this _____ is a factor that affects American behavior, there is also a characteristic pendulum-type movement between the two ethics.

4. If the current trends continue, by 2020, the population of Singapore may start to _____.

5. Concurrent evolution is a form of evolution in which all time space continuums _____ and learn together.

6. China is among several countries in the region that _____ rice prices, an increasingly expensive proposition.

7. Revenue income is receipts from the sale of goods and services, plus other _____ from the operation of the business.

8. Learn to _____ your positive attribute.

9. The future world will be a _____ of human and machine that will generate better and faster decisions anytime, anywhere.

10. Are you _____ tonight?

II. Decide whether the following statements are true (T) or false (F) according to the passage.

1. Ann Moore graduated from Harvard University in 1978. (   )

2. Ann Moore moved to People in 1991, and helped make it one of the most profitable magazines in the world. (   )

3. At some of her magazines, such as Time, advertising revenues are down by around 40% compared with this time last year, according to Media Industry Newsletter. (   )

4. Magazines may indeed be better placed than newspapers to cope with the recession and readers' shift towards the web. (   )

5. Ms. Moore doesn't think her firm can lead the way in this shift from freebies to fees. (   )

III. **Translate the following sentences into Chinese.**
   1. This nifty scheme highlights Time Inc's eagerness to attract readers to its magazines—but its ambivalence about adding a price tag.
   2. Ms. Moore has had to tear up her company's five-year plan and draft a new two-year one instead, focusing on two things: internal reorganization and innovation.
   3. Ms. Moore was "bright, charming, energetic, fun and gutsy" and had the skills to "transform Time Inc from a magazine company to a publishing company" that made its output available online as well as in print.
   4. Another possibility is that readers may be prepared to subscribe to content on portable devices such as Amazon's Kindle e-reader or advanced "smart" phones.
   5. But Mr. Parsons, who has watched her career closely, admits that she is now operating in troubled waters, as she tries to cope with a recession in addition to the rise of the internet.

Supplementary Reading

Steve Jobs and the iPad of Hope
—Apple's Innovation Machine Churns out Another Game-changing Device

"HEROES and heroics" is one of the central themes of the

current season at the Yerba Buena Center for the Arts in San Francisco, which prides itself on showcasing contemporary artists who challenge conventional ways of doing things. On January 27th the centre played host to one of the heroes of the computing industry: Steve Jobs, the boss of Apple, who launched the company's latest creation, the iPad. Mr. Jobs also has a reputation for showcasing the unconventional. He did not disappoint.

The iPad, which looks like an oversized Apple iPhone and boasts a colour screen measuring almost ten inches (25cm), promises to change the landscape of the computing world. It is just half an inch thick and weighs 1.5lb (680 grams). "It's so much more intimate than a laptop, and so much more capable than a smartphone," Mr. Jobs said of the device, which will be available in late March.

The new iPad has important limitations, which critics were quick to point out. It does not have a camera or a phone and users cannot run multiple applications on it at the same time. But Apple should be able to correct such flaws in due course. Together with a host of other touch-screen "tablet" computers that are expected to reach shops over the next year or so, the iPad looks set to revolutionise the way in which digital media are consumed in homes, schools and offices.

The flood of devices is likely to have a profound impact on parts of the media business that are already being turned upside-down by the Internet. The move from print to digital has not been easy for newspaper or magazine publishers. Readers have proved reluctant to pay for content on the web. Companies are unwilling to pay as much for online advertisements as for paper ones—hardly surprising, given the amount of space on offer. The iPad will probably accelerate the shift away from printed matter towards digital content, which could worsen the industry's pain in the short term. Yet publishers hope that tablets will turn out to be the 21st-century equivalent of the printed page, offering them compelling new ways to present their content and to charge for it. "This is really a chance for publishers to seize on a second life," says Phil Asmundson of Deloitte, a consultancy.

It does not come as a surprise, then, that Apple has already attracted some blue-chip media brands to the iPad's platform. During his presentation Mr. Jobs revealed that the company had struck deals with leading publishers such as Penguin and Simon & Schuster. They will provide books for the iPad, to be found and paid for in Apple's new iBooks online store. More agreements ought to be signed before the first iPads are shipped in March. Users will also be able to download applications that give them access to electronic versions of newspapers such as the *New York Times*, which presented an iPad app at the launch.

Apple's media partners no doubt have mixed feelings about dealing with Mr. Jobs. Apple is now widely demonized in the music industry for dominating the digital downloading business with its iTunes store. The firm has been able to control the price of music, boosting sales of iPods but not bringing the record companies a great deal of money. That said, Apple did provide a way for the music business to make a profit online, which had hitherto eluded it. Apple's sleek iPhone has also given plenty of content producers a platform on which they can charge for their wares.

The firm's record suggests that it will be able to make one of the computing industry's most fervent wishes come true. Technology companies have repeatedly tried to make a success of tablets or similar devices. But the zone between laptops and mobile phones has been something of a Bermuda Triangle for device-makers, points out Roger Kay of Endpoint Technologies, a consultancy. "Products launched in there have usually disappeared from the radar screen," he says.

Among them are previous generations of tablet-style computers. In the 1990s various companies experimented with the machines, including Apple. When its Newton personal digital assistant failed to take off, Mr. Jobs killed the project. Tablets were once again briefly in the limelight when Microsoft's Bill Gates predicted they would soon become people's primary computing device—powered, of course, by his company's software. That did not come to pass because consumers were put off by tablets' high prices, clunky user interfaces and limited capabilities. Instead the devices, which cost almost as much as proper PCs, have remained a niche product used primarily in industries such as health care and construction.

Why are tablets causing so much excitement these days? One reason is that innovations in display, battery and microprocessing technologies have greatly reduced their cost. Apple's iPad is priced at between $499 for the basic version and $829 for one with lots of memory and a 3G wireless connection, bringing it within the reach of ordinary consumers. Another reason for optimism is that interfaces have improved greatly. The iPad boasts a big virtual keyboard, which pops up when needed. It also features multi-touch, meaning that two fingers can be used to change the size of a photo. Furthermore, tablets will benefit from the fact that people have become accustomed to buying and consuming content in digital form.

All this explains why other firms are eyeing the tablet market too. Dozens of prototypes were on show at a consumer-electronics trade fair in Las Vegas earlier this month, including ones from Motorola, Lenovo and Dell. Jen-Hsun Huang, the chief executive of NVIDIA, a maker of graphics chips, reckons this is the first time he has seen telecoms firms, computer-makers and consumer-electronics companies all equally keen to produce the same product. "The tablet is the first truly convergent electronic device," he says.

Netbooks and e-books

The iPad and other tablets could shake up the computing scene. There has been some speculation that they could dent sales of low-end PCs, including Apple's MacBook. But a more likely scenario is that they eat into sales of netbooks, the cheap mini-laptops that are used mainly for web surfing and watching videos. Netbooks have been on a roll recently, with global sales rising by 72% to $11.4 billion last year, according to Display Search, a market research company. That makes them a tempting target.

Apple's new device also poses a threat to dedicated e-readers such as Amazon's Kindle, though these will probably remain popular with the most voracious bookworms. Apple's long-expected entry into the tablet market has already forced e-reader firms to consider making their devices more versatile and exciting. "You will see more readers using colour and video over the next five years," predicts Richard Archuleta of Plastic Logic, which produces the Que proReader. And more makers of e-readers may mimic Amazon's recent decision to let third-party developers create software for its line of Kindles.

Book publishers are quietly hoping that Apple's entry into e-books will help to reduce the clout of Amazon: the Kindle has

60% of the e-reader market, according to Forrester, a research firm. They are also excited by the opportunities that tablets offer to combine various media. Bradley Inman, the boss of Vook, a firm that mixes texts with video and links to people's social networks, believes the iPad will trigger an outpouring of creativity. "Its impact will be the equivalent of adding sound to movies or colour to TV," he says.

Newspaper and magazine publishers are also thrilled by tablets' potential. Their big hope is that the devices will allow them to generate revenues both from readers and advertisers. People have proven willing to pay for long-form journalism on e-readers. But these devices do not allow publishers to present their content in creative ways and most cannot carry advertisements. Skiff, a start-up spun out of Hearst, is a rare exception to this rule. Its 11.5-inch reader is large enough to show off all elements of a magazine's design and accommodates advertising too.

Apple's arrival in the tablet market means that publishers will have to develop digital content for these devices, as well as for e-readers and smart-phones. Many will prove unable or unwilling to do so themselves. That may boost firms such as Zinio, which has developed a digital-publishing model called Unity. This takes publications' content, repurposes it for different gadgets and stores it in "the cloud", the term used to describe giant pools of shared data-processing capacity. Users pay once for the content and can access it on various Zinio-enabled devices, increasing the chances that it will be consumed.

Apple has other ambitions for the iPad. It hopes it will become a popular gaming machine and has designed the device so that many of the games among the 140,000 apps available for other Apple products will run on it straight away. The company has also revamped its iWork suite of word-processing, spreadsheet and presentation software for the iPad in an effort to ensure that the new device will catch on with business folk.

Apple's shareholders are no doubt hoping that the iPad will live up to its billing as a seminal device in the history of computing. They have already seen the company's share price soar. Defying the recession, on January 25th Apple announced the best quarterly results in its 34-year history, with revenues rising to $15.7 billion and profits to $3.4 billion—an increase of 32% and 50% respectively over the previous year. They will be keeping their fingers crossed that the iPad turns into another billion-dollar hit rate? Whether or not that turns out to be the case, Mr. Jobs has already proven heroic enough to merit a portrait on the Yerba Buena Center's walls.

Tips

商务英语常用缩写词：

FA (fixed assets)　固定资产

FAF (free at factory)　工厂交货

FAQ (fair average quality)　（货品）中等平均质量

FA (face amount)　票面金额

FAS (free alongside ship)　发运地船边交货价

FAT (fixed asset transfer)　固定资产转移

FAT (factory acceptance test)　工厂验收试验

FB (foreign bank)　外国银行

FBE (foreign bill of exchange)　外国汇票

FC (fixed capital)　固定资本

FC (fixed charges) 固定费用
FC (future contract) 远期合同
FCG (foreign currency guarantee) 外币担保
FCL (full container load) 整货柜装载
FCL/LCL [full container load/less (than) full container load] 整装/分卸
FCR (forwarders cargo receipt) 货运代理行收据
fd. (fund) 资金
FDI (foreign direct investment) 对外直接投资
FE (foreign exchange) 外汇
FE (future exchange) 远期外汇
FIBC (financial institution buyer credit policy) 金融机构买方信贷险
FIFO (first in, first out) 先进先出法
fin. stat. (F/S) financial statement 财务报表
fin. yr. (financial year) 财政年度
FINA (following items not available) 以下项目不可获得
FIO (free in and out) 自由进出
FIT (free of income tax) 免交所得税
FLG (finance lease guarantee) 金融租赁担保
flt. (flat) 无利息
FMV (fair market value) 合理市价
FO (free out) 包括卸货费在内的运费
FOB (free on board) （启运港）船上交货、离岸价格
FOB (airport) （启运）机场交货（价）
FOC (free of charge) 免费
FOCUS (Financial and Operations Combined Uniform Single Report) 财务经营综合报告
FOK (fill or kill) 要么买进或卖出，要么取消
FOR [free on rail (or road)] 铁路或（公路）上交货价
FOREX (foreign exchange) 外汇
FOUO (for official use only) 仅用于公事

FOW (free on wagon)　火车上交货（价）

FOX (Futures and Options Exchange)　期货和期权交易所

frt. /frgt. (forward)　期货、远期合约

Frt. fwd (freight forward)　运费待付

Frt. ppd (freight prepaid)　运费已付

FS (final settlement)　最后结算

FTZ (free trade zone)　自由贸易区

fut.(futures)　期货、将来

FV (face value)　面值

FVA (fair value accounting)　合理价值法

FWD［forward (exchange) contract］　远期合约

FX (foreign exchange)　外汇

FX (broker foreign exchange broker)　外汇经纪人

FXRN (fixed rate note)　定息票据

FY［fiscal year (financial year)］　财政（务）年度

FYI (for your information)　供您参考

FP (fully paid)　已全付的

Unit 4

E-Commerce

Text A In E-Commerce, More Is More

导读：电子商务通常是指在全球各地广泛的商业贸易活动中，在因特网开放的网络环境下，买卖双方不谋面地进行各种商贸活动，实现消费者网上购物、商户之间网上交易和在线电子支付及各种商务活动、交易活动、金融活动和相关综合服务活动的一种新型的商业运营模式。在网络使用频繁的当今社会，电子商务已趋向国际化，成为企业必不可少的营销手段之一。

Many business leaders, disappointed by online sales growth, see Web consumers as disloyal and unwilling to spend. But that's because the managers are not exploiting what customers value most: engagement.

Online automobile shoppers want information about cars, yes, but they also want to learn about such other topics as travel, sports, apparel, and finance, research shows. Online shoppers for upscale clothing might typically want information on art or even business.

Most firms limit their sites to providing narrow information about the products or services that are for sale. Indeed, the majority of managers we spoke to in our global study told us they believe that a broad array of information diverts attention from the core offerings. But we found it helps customers search for solutions, invites them to think of all the ways the core products might add value to their lives, wins their loyalty, and entices them to buy. In fact, we found that exploiting consumers' desire for engagement is the single dominant driver of superior shareholder value for e-commerce companies.

Our research involved an analysis of more than 1,700 e-commerce sites, along with interviews of 238 consumers and 112 managers in the United States, Europe, and Asia over four years. Some 57% of the managers were disappointed by their firms' online sales growth, but only 17% had a plan to change their sites to improve sales—an indication that they didn't even know how to start turning things around. Most believed that price was the only important way to attract online customers.

We scored the sites on the five practices that customers said they cared about most, and we found that a higher overall ranking on those practices is associated with greater company value, as measured by Tobin's Q, the ratio of market value to asset replacement value. In addition, the shares of the 25 companies with the highest-ranking sites outperformed the S&P 500 by two percentage points, on an annual basis, from 2003 through 2006.

Four of the practices are increasingly common and expected by consumers—without them, sites can't hope to keep buyers around long. They are: personalized shopping, clear categorization, order tracking, and in-depth products or service-related information. It's the fifth practice—customer engagement through the provision of information on related products and services—that represents the most significant opportunity. A high ranking on this practice is a stronger predictor of the company's Tobin's Q than the rankings of any of the other four. The top 25 companies for customer engagement outperformed the S&P 500 by more than 12 percentage points, on an annual basis, throughout the period. Only about 23% of the sites in our sample made use of customer engagement practices.

What Engages Online Shoppers Most

Ralph Lauren's e-commerce site is a good example of how to engage users. Through the online "luxury lifestyle" *RL Magazine*, consumers are invited to regularly revisit the site to learn about fashion, art, sports, healthy diets, and business—facilitating brand attachments and associations that go beyond the core product. Corporate performance reflects the success of the e-commerce site: The firm's Tobin's Q increased from 1.6 in 2003 to 2.6 in 2006, and its stock price more than tripled from 2003 to 2007.

One very effective way for a company to start learning what its customers are interested in is to offer Web visitors a wide list of topics and ask them to vote on which they like. The firm can use those responses to help it decide which attributes—wealth, attractiveness, exclusivity, for instance—it wants customers to associate with its brand. The next step is to provide supplementary information that will help customers make those associations. Porsche, for example, uses the Web to offer adventure tours and travel information, reinforcing the brand's image of passion and high performance.

Focus on Four Basic Needs of Online Customers

One significant part of a strategic plan is the way in which a firm will develop relationships with new customers. One way to initiate the customer service aspect of an e-commerce strategic plan is to consider four basic needs of virtual customers: information, security, support, and privacy.

E-Customers Need Information. Information access is the driving force of e-commerce. The Internet is particularly effective in providing customers with the information needed to compare products or services, to research a manufacturer, and to select a provider. The challenge is to deliver this information conveniently. Site design and functionality are the online equivalent of an attractive showroom and professional sales staff.

One clear key to success in online sales is prominent positioning on Internet search engines such as Yahoo!, Excite, Lycos, and AltaVista. These services are the gatekeepers of the electronic marketplace. A consultant may be useful in helping to position a firm prominently in search listings. Search services organize their listings based on factors such as hit count and the way in which keywords are used in the site's title, contents, and coding. But often listings are counterintuitive. Popular sites, such as *Walmart. com* and *Amazon. com*, do not always appear high in the subject listings for their market segments.

E-mail is another way of initiating online communication with prospects. The Los Angeles Times and the Harvard Business Review are examples of companies that send periodic E-mail to prospects. They strategically place bits of news and information in the message along with a commercial offer. Both of these companies also know that it's good business to give prospects the option of excusing themselves from future e-mailings. If they so desire, E-mail is very cost-effective. It costs about $9 to send an E-mail message to 1,200 prospects while the cost of sending a direct mailing or fax to the same audience is some $1,600.

E-Customers Need Security. How secure are Internet transactions? Widespread security concerns linger among consumers despite published improvements in the online processing of credit card information. One recent survey found that 65% of U. S. consumers believe it is unsafe to take part in e-commerce. Another survey found that just 5% of Internet users would risk sending credit card information over open lines.

E-businesses utilize a variety of security methods and often provide general descriptions of these measures on their web sites to assure customers that personal information is protected. Progressive companies guarantee that customers will not be liable for any fraudulent activity resulting from online purchases. Their sites often contain general descriptions of encrypting systems or other safeguards in place to protect credit card information.

E-Customers Need Support. The Internet provides new ways of developing closer relationships with customers. Such techniques replicate face to face interactions in important ways. E-mail and messaging are forms of communication that can be used to better understand customer needs. The opportunity for customers to provide feedback to a firm over the Internet can establish two-way relationships and help build customer trust. Return policies are also important.

Many firms offer full refunds on goods returned in original condition. With such assurance of satisfaction, customers will make online transactions more readily. Still, the extent to which customer loyalty exists on the Internet is yet to be seen.

E-Customers Need Privacy. Finally, customers need assurance that online firms will not disclose personal information to other parties. If the Internet is to remain a largely self-policing entity, firms must refrain from selling or exchanging customer names and demographic data. Customers will quickly abandon firms when such abuses are discovered.

E-commerce offers significant opportunities and challenges to firms in traditional markets as well as in newly emerging ones. The genie is out of the bottle and can no longer be ignored. Managers have an obligation to explore new ways of serving customers, suppliers, and other stakeholders. Time is of the essence. As Harry Newton stated in a recent issue of Computer Telephony, "If your company is not getting ready for the explosion of Web business, you're road kill. Period."

Notes:

1. **Lycos（搜索引擎名）:** a search engine and web portal established in 1994. Lycos also encompasses a network of Email, webhosting, social networking, and entertainment websites.

2. **Excite（搜索引擎名）:** an Internet portal, and as one of the major "dotcom portals" of the 1990s (along with Yahoo!, Lycos and Netscape), it was once one of the most recognized brands on the Internet. Today it offers a variety of services, including search, web-based Email, instant messaging, stock quotes, and a customizable user homepage.

3. **AltaVista（搜索引擎名）:** a Web search engine owned by Yahoo! AltaVista was once one of the most popular search engines but its popularity declined with the rise of Google.

4. **Computer telephony integration（CTI）（电脑电话整合技术）:** a kind of technology that allows interactions on a telephone and a computer to be integrated or co-ordinated.

Words & Expressions:

1. divert [dai'və:t] *vt.* 转移；使……欢娱；使……转向
   vi. 转移
2. shareholder ['ʃeəhəuldə] *n.* 股东；股票持有人
   substantial shareholder 大股东；主要股东
   significant shareholder 重要股东；持有大量股票的股东

equity shareholder 普通股股东；普通股持有者

3. categorization [kætigəri'zeiʃən] n. 分类；分门别类；编目方法
4. exclusivity [eksklu:'sivəti] n. 排外性；独占权
   market exclusivity 市场专属权
   exclusivity agreement 独家经营；排他性协议
5. counterintuitive [kauntərin'tju:itiv] adj. 违反直觉的
6. transaction [træn'zækʃən] n. 交易；事务；办理；会报，学报
7. fraudulent ['frɔ:djulənt] adj. 欺骗性的；不正的
   fraudulent signature 欺诈性签名
   fraudulent device 诈性行为
8. encrypt [in'kript] vt. 将……译成密码
9. replicate ['replikit] vt. 复制；折叠
                         vi. 重复；折转
                         adj. 复制的；折叠的
                         n. 复制品；八音阶间隔的反复音
10. demographic [demə'græfik] adj. 人口统计学的；人口学的
11. obligation [ɔbli'geiʃən] n. 义务；职责；债务

Exercises:

I. **Fill in the blanks with the suitable words given in the box. Change the form when necessary.**

| divert | encrypt | transaction | exclusivity |
| replication | fraudulent | categorize | obligation |

1. Egypt is building 20 new cities _____ people away from Cairo.
2. He urged everybody, his colleagues, to follow China's lead and _____ their success.
3. Businesses need to update security software, _____ data and be aware of data flow.

4. The Kazakh authorities believe many of the loans made by BTA management were _____.

5. Following the _____, Li Hanchun's stake in the company fell to 2.46% from 3.9%.

6. In information retrieval, a word used to _____ or index information.

7. Our goal is to create a culture of _____ and develop a reputation as a market leader.

8. We have one short life, are given certain resources and have an _____ to use them.

II. **Decide whether the following statements are true (T) or false (F) according to the passage.**

1. A large number of firms adopt the measure of limiting their sites to providing narrow information about the products or services because they believe that is a good way to gain focus for their products. (   )

2. It is believed that the "Four of the practices", which become increasingly common and expected by consumers, represent the most significant opportunity. (   )

3. Learning about what customers are interested in and thus subsequently providing supplementary information are two effective ways for firms to adopt in order to attract customers' attention. (   )

4. An attractive showroom and professional sales staff in real life would work better than on-line site design and functionality. (   )

5. By writing *"The genie is out of the bottle and can no longer be ignored."* the writer means companies need to take efforts to make themselves more adjustable and flexible to embrace the changes in the newly emerging markets. (   )

III. **Topic discussion.**

1. Discuss with your partner and make a summary of the basic issues for firms to consider when developing an e-commerce plan according to the text.

2. Suppose you are the marketing manager in a large company, what are the appropriate methods you would like to adopt to extend your business on line?

3. In your perspective, what did Harry Newton mean when he said, "If your company is not getting ready for the explosion of web business, you're road kill."?

Text B　The Alibaba E-Commerce Empire

> 导读：阿里巴巴是全球企业间电子商务的著名品牌，是目前全球最大的网上交易市场和商务交流社区。阿里巴巴创建于1998年年底，总部设在杭州，并在海外美国硅谷、伦敦等设立分支机构。阿里巴巴由于其良好的定位、稳固的结构、优秀的服务两次被哈佛大学商学院选为MBA案例，在美国学术界掀起研究热潮，四次被美国权威财经杂志《福布斯》选为全球最佳B2B网站之一，多次被相关机构评为全球最受欢迎的B2B网站、中国商务类优秀网站、中国百家优秀网站、中国最佳贸易网站。国内外媒体和国外风险投资家称它为与Zgsyw, Yahoo, Amazon, eBay, AOL比肩的六大互联网商务流派代表之一。

If there is one Chinese Internet company CEO that you need recognize it is Jack Ma, founder of Alibaba Group. Ma, named one of the world's 30 best CEOs this past March, started off as an English teacher. However, in 1999 he founded Alibaba out of his Hangzhou apartment with about ＄60,000 determined to build a bridge between Chinese small to medium manufacturers and foreign buyers around the world. Alibaba Group is now the largest e-commerce company in all of China and is a global e-commerce leader.

Alibaba.com—Global B2B marketplace

Alibaba.com Limited (HKSE: 1688) is the world's leading B2B e-commerce company. It connects millions of buyers and suppliers from around the world every day through three marketplaces: an English-language marketplace for global

importers and exporters, a Chinese-language marketplace for domestic trade in China, and, through a joint venture, a Japanese-language marketplace facilitating trade to and from Japan. Together, the marketplaces form a community of 36 million registered users from over 240 countries and regions.

Taobao—China's largest consumer e-commerce company (Comparable to Ebay)

Taobao (taobao.com) is the largest online shopping marketplace for consumers in China. With a registered user base of more than 80 million as of September 2008, Taobao reaches an overwhelming majority of online shoppers in China. In 2007, Taobao's transaction volume, or gross merchandise volume (GMV), was ¥43.3 billion, up 156% year-on-year. In the first half of 2008, Taobao's GMV was ¥41.3 billion. Since its launch in 2003, Taobao has grown into an ecosystem where over 1 million online merchants reach a growing online consumer population in China.

Alibaba, China's largest online advertising exchange platform, was combined with Taobao in September 2008. Alibaba helps China's more than 1 million small and medium-size websites, which generate an estimated 80% of China's Internet traffic, to sell online advertising inventory and monetize their traffic. It currently serves 3 billion ad impressions that reach 80 million consumers every day. Launched in November 2007, Alibaba's network currently includes 400,000 web publishers and advertisers.

Alipay—Safe and secure online payment (Comparable to Paypal)

Alipay (alipay.com) is China's leading online payment service, enabling individuals and businesses to execute payments online in an easy, safe and secure manner. Founded in 2004 by Alibaba Group, Alipay is the designated online payment service provider for Taobao and Alibaba.com's China marketplace, as well as a widely-accepted online payment method for retail websites and other Internet businesses in China. Alipay partners with domestic PRC banks to provide an escrow service for payments, which reduces the settlement risk faced by

Alipay's customers in their e-commerce transactions.

In August 2007, Alipay launched an online payment solution to help merchants worldwide sell directly to consumers in China and now cooperates with over 300 global retail brands and supports transactions in 12 major foreign currencies. At the end of August 2008, Alipay facilitated 2 million transactions each day with a registered user base of over 100 million and daily payment volume of ￥450 million.

Yahoo! Koubei—Online classified listings for local services and search

Yahoo! Koubei is a trusted platform connecting Chinese Internet users to their local communities, their interests and the information they need to inspire their lives. It operates two websites: China Yahoo! (yahoo.com.cn), a leading Chinese language portal and search engine in China, and Yahoo! Koubei (koubei.com), China's leading classified listing website providing consumers with local information on various topics, including real estate, restaurants, travel, entertainment and employment.

In October 2005, Alibaba Group acquired China Yahoo! in a transaction whereby Yahoo! Inc. became a substantial shareholder of Alibaba Group. Yahoo! Koubei (then called "Koubei.com") became part of Alibaba Group in 2006 through a strategic investment. The China Yahoo! and Yahoo! Koubei businesses were integrated in June 2008.

Alibaba Cloud Computing

Alibaba Cloud Computing aims to build an advanced data-centric cloud computing service platform, including e-commerce data mining, high-speed massive e-commerce data processing, as well as data customization. It was established in September 2009 in conjunction with the company's 10th anniversary.

Notes:

1. **Alibaba Group**（阿里巴巴集团）: a privately owned Hangzhou-based family of Internet-based businesses that includes business-to-business international trade, online retail and

payment platforms and data-centric cloud computing services. It was founded by Ma Yun in 1999.

2. Business-to-Business (B2B)（企业对企业）: describes commerce transactions between businesses, such as between a manufacturer and a wholesaler, or between a wholesaler and a retailer. Contrasting terms are business-to-consumer (B2C) and business-to-government (B2G).

3. Ebay（易趣）: an American Internet company that manages eBay. com, an online auction and shopping website in which people and businesses buy and sell a broad variety of goods and services worldwide. Founded in 1995, ebay is one of the notable success stories of the dot-com bubble; it is now a multi-billion dollar business with operations localized in over thirty countries.

4. PayPal（贝宝：全球最大的在线支付平台）: an e-commerce business allowing payments and money transfers to be made through the Internet. PayPal serves as an electronic alternative to traditional paper methods such as checks and money orders.

Words & Expressions：

1. marketplaces ['mɑːkitpleis] n. 市场；商场；市集
2. joint venture 合资企业；联合经营
3. register ['redʒistə] vt. 登记；注册；记录；挂号邮寄；把……挂号；正式提出
   vi. 登记；注册；挂号
   n. 登记；注册；记录；寄存器；登记簿
4. GMV:（Gross Merchandise Volume）总交易额；总商品量
5. monetize ['mʌnitaiz] vt. 定为货币，使成为合法货币；铸造成货币
6. substantial [səb'stænʃəl] adj. 大量的；实质的；内容充实的
   n. 本质；重要材料

7. customization [ˌkʌstəmaiˈzeiʃən] n. 定制；[计] 用户化；定制化服务
8. escrow [ˈeskrəu] n. 由第三者保存附带条件委付盖印的契约
   vt. 把……暂交第三者保管以待条件实现

Exercises:

Ⅰ. Fill in the blanks with the suitable words given in the box. Change the form when necessary.

| register | substantial | monetize | joint |
| auction | transfer | escrow | payment |

1. We have had a very happy start, and I believe this can lead to more _____ business between us.
2. They promote or _____ employees on the basis of seniority.
3. Once you have a flat in central Berlin, you can always _____ it when the prices rise.
4. If you _____ on line we will contact you with your access details.
5. The car seller agreed to _____ the sum of $2,000 with her attorney.

Ⅱ. Read the following text and choose the best answers to fill in each of the gaps.

Research has shown that in today's dynamic working environment the traditional job description is no longer doing its job. Today's jobs are not (1) _____, they are constantly changing. This leads to (2) _____, with employees uncertain of their precise work roles. This can be illustrated by the following quotation from a job description: "Meet or exceed customer (3) _____." The initial reaction may be that this (4) _____ is perfectly clear but on closer examination it poses a number of question. For example, is it (5) _____ employees to do whatever they feel is necessary to (6) _____ this end without restrictions? Or is it saying (7) _____ our procedures and this will be the outcome? Who knows? Perhaps the manager, but the description certainly does not (8) _____ things sufficiently from the employee's point of view.

1. A. static   B. routine   C. standard
2. A. disparity   B. initiative   C. ambiguity
3. A. undertakings B. objectives   C. expectations
4. A. schedule   B. feedback   C. statement
5. A. authorizing B. allocating   C. prescribing
6. A. support   B. achieve   C. carry out
7. A. follow   B. comply   C. serve
8. A. highlight   B. identify   C. clarify

Ⅲ. Translate the following phrases into English.

1. 兼并
2. 控制股
3. 上市公司
4. 欧洲债券市场
5. 综合账户
6. 贸易壁垒
7. 进口替代
8. 清算机制
9. 品牌认同
10. 市场准入
11. 专营商店
12. 扣除通货膨胀后的收入
13. 银行间同业拆借市场

Supplementary Reading

Online Shopping: Selling Becomes Sociable

Those who cherish privacy will recoil in horror, but for digital exhibitionists it is a dream. At Swipely, a web start-up, users can now publish their purchases. Whenever they swipe their credit or debit card, the transaction is listed on the site—to be discussed by other users. "Turn purchases into conversations" is the firm's mantra.

Swipely is among the latest entrants in the growing field of social commerce. Firms in this market combine e-commerce with social networks and other online group activities. They aim to transform shopping both online and off. Angus Davis, Swipely's  boss, points out that the Internet has already disrupted the content industry. Commerce will be next, he says.

The first generation of e-commerce sites, which hit the web in the late 1990s, were essentially digitized mail-order catalogues. Websites like Epinions collected user reviews and recommendations, but they did not sell anything—and many collapsed during the dotcom crash. Only Amazon brought together selling and social feedback, to great effect. By means of collective filtering, it made suggestions based on other buyers' purchases.

The second generation of e-commerce firms is quite different. Few emerged from Silicon Valley. Indeed, they tend to have offline roots, and sometimes seek to drive customers to actual shops. Many make their money from flash sales—brief offers of steep discounts on products—that are advertised to registered members.

The pioneer of flash sales, Vente Privée, grew out of the French apparel industry (the name means "private sale"). Even today, its centre of gravity is offline, says Jacques-Antoine Granjon, Vente Privée's boss, who founded the firm in 2001 along with seven partners. Hundreds of designers, photographers and hairstylists organize its online sales events. After a slow start, Vente Privée has been growing quickly. Its five local sites in Europe have more than 12m members and are expected to bring in about 800m ($1 billion) in revenues this year.

Vente Privée's success has inspired others. The best known is Gilt Groupe, which emulates the sample sales of luxury retailers in New York, where it is based. Gilt Groupe is straying into the territory of another clutch of city-based e-commerce sites, which facilitate collective buying. Every day these sites offer the service of a local business—a restaurant meal, a spa-treatment, the rental of an expensive car—at a discount of up to 90% (they generally keep half of the sale price). But a deal is struck only if a minimum number of members pounce. Buyers thus have an interest in spreading the word, which they do mostly on social networks.

Many such sites have sprung up. The most successful is

Groupon (a combination of the words "group" and "coupon", which buyers print out to pay for their service). Although the firm launched only in late 2008, it already operates some 230 local websites in 29 countries and boasts 15m subscribers. Flush with money from investors, it has embarked on a global land-grab, buying Groupon clones in other countries, such as Germany's CityDeal.

Groupon is more about people than technology. It grew out of The Point, a Chicago-based website that offers tools to organize collective action. The firm employs a worldwide sales force of nearly 2000 to identify interesting local merchants and 150 writers to describe the offers. It wants to be the company that finally allows small businesses to participate in e-commerce, explains Rob Solomon, its president.

For the new generation of e-commerce firms, the offline world is as important as the online one. Swipely is a good example. By uploading transaction data, the start-up makes it easy for customers to tell their friends how they are spending their money in the real world, something they probably would not do if they had to type all the data in. At the same time, customers can keep those transactions secret that they do not want to share.

Will making shopping more social really disrupt commerce as much as Mr. Davis expects? It is hard to predict whether the second and third generations of e-commerce sites will continue their rapid growth. Consumers may tire of flash sales, as they did of online auctions. Even collective buying may have its limits. One of Groupon's biggest problems is that tens of thousands of local firms want to be featured, but each of its sites offers only one deal per day. The outfit has started to personalize some of its sites, meaning that different users will see different deals depending on things like age, sex and interests. But if personalization goes too far, and users see only the sort of things they already knew they wanted, this kind of shopping could become less fun.

Whatever the fate of individual firms and sales models, e-commerce is bound to become more social, predicts Sonali de Rycker of Accel Partners, a venture-capital firm. Retailing has several persistent problems: the high cost of attracting visitors, the low probability that they become buyers and the difficulty of getting them to come back. Sociable e-commerce offers potential solutions to all of them. So expect your favorite site to add social features, whereas many of the pioneers will end up with arrows in their backs, as innovators often do.

Tips

常用电子商务词汇：

    authentication   身份认证
    certification authority (CA)   认证机构
    advance notification of payment   支付前通知
    advance shipment notice (ASN)   装运前通知
    automated clearing houses (ACH)   自动交换中心
    automated teller machine (ATM)   自动取款机
    bar coding   条码
    blind signature   伪签名
    gateway   网关
    e-wallet   电子钱包
    cash concentration and disbursement (CCD)   资金集中与支付
    clipper chip   审查芯片
    commerce net   商务网
    consumer EDI   消费者电子数据交换

continuous replenishment (CR)　持续更新
corporate trade exchange (CTX)　公司交易汇兑
corporate trade payments (CTP)　公司交易支付
costs of EDI　电子数据交换成本
credit cards　信用卡
currency server　货币服务器
data encryption standard (DES)　数据编码加密标准
debit cards　计账卡
digital cash　数字化现金
digital signature　数字化签名
disbursement services　支付服务
disintermediation　非居间化
double spending　重复付款
EDIBANX　电子数据交换银行联合网络交易
EDI gateways　电子数据交换网关
EDI hubs　电子数据交换集线器
EDI translation software　电子数据交换翻译软件
efficient consumer response (ECR)　消费者有效应答
e-cash　电子现金
e-catalogs　电子商品目录
e-checks　电子支票

Unit 5

Economic Globalization and Multinational Corporation

Text A   Globalization vs. Economic Sovereignty

> **导读**：自21世纪起，各国开始加速经济开放速度，世界经济一体化趋势愈演愈烈。但是，对于任何一个国家来说，对外开放经济、投身世界市场从来就不是一顿"免费的午餐"。经济全球化带来的后果之一就是各国经济主权的相对让步，有些不发达国家为了参与世界经济，甚至需要其他国家的经济支援与干预。有些经济学家认为"经济全球化"将世界带入了"新殖民主义"时代，但也有一些经济学家认为各国在参与世界经济的同时，能够建立新的国际经济体制，形成"结构化权力"。

Almost all countries in the world have accelerated their tempo of economic opening up since the beginning of the 21st century.

With the initiative, they expect to inject a new driving force into domestic economic development, and to create new market opportunities. They hope to integrate their domestic economy into the global market, and to develop economic muscles that can punch a worldwide weight.

However, for any country, opening the economy to the outside world is by no means a free lunch. The policy will inevitably come at a cost.

The cost can be perceived to be a weakening of the nation's "economic sovereignty," namely the erosion of permanent and exclusive privileges over its economic activities, wealth, and natural resources.

A review of the world's history will find it is common that economic sovereignty of an individual member is from time to time influenced by global economic trends.

The increase of the number of international organizations and the expansion of their functions has undeniably restricted an individual country's sovereignty to certain extent.

The most typical example is the increasingly extensive involvement of the world's three leading financial institutions the World Bank (WB), the International Momentary Fund (IMF) and the World Trade Organization (WTO) in domestic economic affairs of their members.

The 60,000-plus transnational corporations, which developed rapidly in the latter half of the last century, are now sharing or "encroaching upon" individual country's "sovereignty" in the economic domain.

Owing to disorderly domestic economic establishments, many underdeveloped nations even have to resort to foreign assistance and intervention, leading to their governments being deprived of the control of their own economy.

Due to this, some scholars predicted the loss of their economic sovereignty under this form of neo-colonialism. More importantly, some of the world's leading economic entities, such as the United States, the European Union and Japan, by taking advantage of their predominant economic status, are affecting or infringing upon other countries' economic sovereignty.

Under these circumstances, an increasing number of scholars have concluded that the economic dominion of individual nations has come to an end.

Basing this assertion upon the penetrating systems and rules of the world's financial

organs, some of them insist on a kind of theory such as state economic sovereignty being eroded. Some deny the long-existed doctrine of the "national entity being in a central position," by citing trade liberalization and economic integration tendency and thus advocate "ambiguity of economic sovereignty."

Also, some even assert that in the greater globalization picture, a country's economic sovereignty should be discarded and state sovereignty should be replaced by supranational law.

As the academic debate of the economic rights of a state reaches boiling point, the era of globalization begins.

However, while stressing the possibility of a nation's economic sovereignty being enfeebled in the course of economic globalization, many of these scholars have obviously forgotten that individual nations also have the ability to produce and mould international frameworks, rules, systems and orders, the ability that has been called a "structural power."

Late British international economist Susan Strange believed that this kind of power is embodied in the four basic international structures which are the security, knowledge, production and financial, as well as in some sub-structures such as trade.

After an analysis of the "structural power," we can see that in the economic globalization era, sovereign states have never lost control of their sovereignty. The power of international economic organizations originates from its transfer from individual members in the world community. And their birth is exactly the product of sovereign states' self-restriction and self-restraints in the economic realm.

Also, economic activities of transnational corporations have not brought about any essential restrictions on state sovereignty of individual nations.

So far, transnational corporations have not changed their legal status as legal entities under the jurisdiction of the state. And their worldwide business activities also have not changed individual countries' right to exercise their full sovereignty.

For this, the United States' move to disintegrate the Microsoft corporation years ago could serve as an example. Despite its economic strength being even larger than a number of individual nations, the world's largest software producer still lacked an effective means to influence American economic sovereignty.

Possibly, for the ones who strongly advocate the "end of economic sovereignty," the most convincing evidence is the debilitating of sovereignty of a host of economically weak nations.

However, this phenomenon is just the product of developed nations' unfair treatment of developing nations in the era of economic globalization.

Most of the time, developed countries turn to double standards in economic affairs and apply their self-concocted theories like "human rights being superior to sovereignty" and "economic integration outweighing sovereignty" to force weak nations into conceding some of their inherent privileges. However, these countries repeatedly stress that they should not accept international economic regulations at the sacrifice of weakening, infringing upon, and harming their own decision-making rights.

Thus, it can be concluded that the dispute about economic sovereignty is essentially a hidden power struggle on the world stage. Under the current context of "economic openness," outside economic influences upon individual nations are distributed in an unbalanced manner. Similarly, their ability to weaken the economic sovereignty of different nations also varies.

Notes:

1. **The World Bank（世界银行, 缩写为 WB）:** The World Bank is an international financial institution that provides loans to developing countries for capital programmes. The World Bank has a goal of reducing poverty. By law, all of its decisions must be guided by a commitment to promote foreign investment, international trade and facilitate capital investment. The World Bank differs from the World Bank Group, in that the World Bank comprises only two institutions: the International Bank for Reconstruction and Development (IBRD) and the International Development Association (IDA), whereas the latter incorporates these two in addition to three more: International Finance Corporation (IFC), Multilateral Investment Guarantee Agency (MIGA), and International Centre for Settlement of Investment Disputes (ICSID).

2. **The International Monetary Fund（国际货币基金组织, 缩写为 IMF）:** The International Monetary Fund (IMF) is the intergovernmental organization that oversees the global financial system by following the macroeconomic policies of its member countries, in particular those with an impact on exchange rate and the balance of payments. It is an organization formed with a stated objective of stabilizing international exchange rates and facilitating development through the enforcement of liberalizing economic policies on other countries as a condition for loans, restructuring or aid. It also offers loans with varying levels of conditionality, mainly to poorer countries. Its headquarters are in

Washington, D. C., United States. The IMF's relatively high influence in world affairs and development has drawn heavy criticism from some sources.

3. **The World Trade Organization（世界贸易组织，缩写为WTO）**: The World Trade Organization (WTO) is an organization that intends to supervise and liberalize international trade. The organization officially commenced on January 1, 1995 under the Marrakech Agreement, replacing the General Agreement on Tariffs and Trade (GATT), which commenced in 1948. The organization deals with regulation of trade between participating countries; it provides a framework for negotiating and formalizing trade agreements, and a dispute resolution process aimed at enforcing participants' adherence to WTO agreements which are signed by representatives of member governments and ratified by their parliaments. The WTO has 153 members, representing more than 97% of total world trade and 30 observers, most seeking membership. The WTO is governed by a ministerial conference, meeting every two years; a general council, which implements the conference's policy decisions and is responsible for day-to-day administration; and a director-general, who is appointed by the ministerial conference. The WTO's headquarters is at the Centre William Rappard, Geneva, Switzerland.

4. **The European Union（欧盟，缩写为EU）**: The European Union (EU) is an economic and political union of 27 member states which are located primarily in Europe. The EU traces its origins from the European Coal and Steel Community (ECSC) and the European Economic Community (EEC) formed by six countries in the 1950s. In the intervening years the EU has grown in size by the accession of new member states, and in power by the addition of policy areas to its remit. The Maastricht Treaty established the European Union under its current name in 1993.

5. **Susan Strange（苏珊·斯特兰奇）**: Susan Strange（June 9, 1923—October 25, 1998）was a British academic who was influential in the field of international political economy. Her most important publications include *Casino Capitalism, Mad Money, States and Markets* and *The retreat of the State: The Diffusion of Power in the World Economy*. For a

quarter of a century, Susan Strange was the most influential figure in British international studies. She held a number of key academic posts in Britain, Italy and Japan. From 1978 to 1988, she was Montague Burton Professor of International Relations at the London School of Economics and Political Science (LSE), the first woman to hold this chair and a professorial position in international relations at the LSE. She was a major figure in the professional associations of both Britain and the U. S.: she was an instrumental founding member and first Treasurer of the British International Studies Association (BISA) and the first female President of the International Studies Association (ISA) in 1995. Between 1989 and 1994 she was Professor of International Political Economy at the European University Institute in Florence.

Words & Expressions:

1. sovereignty [ˈsɔvrənti] n. 主权；主权国家；君主；独立国
2. integrate [ˈintigreit] vt. 使……完整；使……成整体
3. punch [pʌntʃ] n. 冲压机；打洞器；钻孔机
   vt. 开洞；以拳重击
   vi. 用拳猛击
4. perceive [pəˈsiːv] vt. 察觉，感觉；理解；认知
   vi. 感到，感知；认识到
5. permanent [ˈpəːmənənt] adj. 永久的，永恒的；不变的
6. undeniably [ˌʌndiˈnaiəbli] adv. 不可否认地；确凿无疑地
7. transnational [trænzˈnæʃənəl] adj. 跨国的；超越国界的
8. encroach [inˈkrəutʃ] vi. 侵占；蚕食；侵蚀
   vt. 侵犯
9. resort [riˈzɔːt] vi. 求助，诉诸；常去；采取某手段或方法
10. neo-colonialism [ˌniəkəˈlɔnIəˌlIzəm] n. 新殖民主义
11. entity [ˈentəti] n. 实体；存在；本质

12. predominant [ˌpriˈdɔminənt] adj. 主要的；卓越的；支配的；有力的；有影响的
13. infringe [inˈfrindʒ] vt. 侵犯；违反；破坏
    vi. 侵犯；侵害
14. dominion [dəˈminjən] n. 主权，统治权；支配；领土
15. penetrating [ˈpenitreitiŋ] adj. 渗透的；尖锐的；有洞察力的
16. doctrine [ˈdɔktrin] n. 主义；学说；教义；信条
17. liberalization [ˌlibərəlaiˈzeiʃən] n. 自由化；自由主义化；放宽限制
18. ambiguity [ˌæmbiˈgju:iti] n. 含糊；不明确；暧昧；模棱两可的话
19. supranational [ˌsju:prəˈnæʃənəl] adj. 超国家的；超民族的
20. enfeeble [inˈfi:bl] vt. 使衰弱；使无力
21. mould [məuld] vt. 浇铸；用泥土覆盖
    vi. 发霉
22. jurisdiction [ˌdʒuərisˈdikʃən] n. 司法权，审判权，管辖权；权限，权力
23. debilitate [diˈbiliteit] vt. 使衰弱；使虚弱
24. concoct [kənˈkɔkt] vt. 捏造；混合而制；调合；图谋

Exercises:

I. Fill in the blanks with the suitable words or expressions given in the box. Change the form when necessary.

| by no means | at a cost | to certain extent | encroach upon | owing to |
| resort to | deprive of | at the sacrifice of | infringe upon | come to an end |

1. The modern market-oriented economy may be called the Corporation Economy_____.
2. If other means fail, they will _____ force.
3. Like it or not, _____ the fast pace of progress in the world of computers, obsolescence is almost built into today's technological products, just as it was built into yesterday's.
4. How did we get so terribly rushed in a world saturated with work and responsibility,

yet somehow _____ joy and delight?

5. This was the bloodiest attack in a month but it was _____ unusual.

6. Everybody have privacy, we should punish that _____ others' privacy.

7. But these commitments _____, in part since the companies must pull the troubled loans from mortgage securities and recognize a loss.

8. The irony in his proposal is that such a guest-worker programme would necessarily _____ a federal prerogative.

9. The Congress _____ of their one-month holiday and start afresh working this afternoon.

10. You should never try to earn money _____ your health.

Ⅱ. Translate the following phrases into Chinese or English.
   1. economic sovereignty
   2. domestic economic development
   3. the global market
   4. the latter half of the last century
   5. underdeveloped nations
   6. 对外援助和干预
   7. 经济实体
   8. 主要经济地位
   9. 经济一体化趋势
   10. 决策权

Ⅲ. Topic discussion.
   1. What's the meaning of "economic sovereignty"?
   2. How do you understand "develop economic muscles that can punch a worldwide weight" in Para. 2?
   3. How do you explain "structural power"?
   4. Do you agree that sovereign states will lose control of their sovereignty in the economic globalization era? Why?
   5. After reading this report, what do you think of "economic globalization"?

Text B The World's Top Choice
—China Remains the Most Popular Destination for Foreign Direct Investment

> **导读**：20世纪最后十年，中国吸引了大批跨国公司来华投资。2001年，中国加入WTO，对世界经济的参与度也越来越高。中国成了许多世界大型跨国公司发展经济的首选之地。各大跨国公司在发展经济的同时也繁荣了中国经济市场、为中国经济的发展做出了贡献。

The year 1992 marked major shifts in both the China strategy of attracting foreign investment and multinationals' investment strategies in China, said Wang Zhile, a researcher on multinational corporations, in his report on multinationals and China's three-decade reform and opening up.

China seized the opportunities when multinationals relocated their factories worldwide, thanks to China's decision to establish a socialist market economy in 1992, said Wang.

After 1992, trailblazer multinationals began to expand their investments in China and many countries' top 20 industrial companies set up factories in China, investing in more and bigger projects. During the second period (1992—2001), China attracted $370.2 billion FDI in total.

China's entry into the WTO in 2001 marked a milestone in China's reform and opening up, and also turned a new page for FDI in China, said Wang in the report. Paid-in FDI in China stood at about $561.75 billion from 2002 to 2009, according to MOFCOM statistics.

Diversity—In the past decade, multinationals increased and diversified their investments in China, investing in R&D, product design, and services such as logistics, marketing, wholesale and retail trade, banking and insurance, according to Wang's report. They also invested in fundamental industries such as core raw materials and parts for their productions in China.

By the end of 2007, multinational companies had established more than 1 200 R&D centers, mainly in Beijing, Shanghai, Tianjin, Jiangsu and Guangdong. The R&D technical service sector attracted FDI of $917 million in 2007, up from $57 million in 2000, said MOFCOM statistics.

"Large multinationals, especially Fortune 500 companies, have been establishing more or upgrading their R&D in China into global R&D centers in recent years," said Du Debin, dean of city and regional economics with Shanghai-based East China Normal University in a *China Business News report*.

Multinationals' investments in their China R&D centers had increased 33.3 percent annually between 2004 and 2006, Du said, citing MOFCOM statistics from a survey on 75 multinationals.

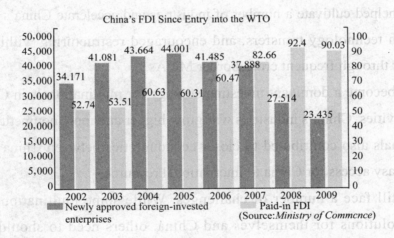

From 1997 to July 2010, FDI in China's service sector stood at $267.9 billion, accounting for 32.4 percent of the total amount, according to MOFCOM statistics.

In recent years, foreign investors also went on an acquisition spree for Chinese companies. A total of 863 cases of mergers and acquisitions (M&As) were approved in 2009, up 1.9 percent year on year, accounting for 3.6 percent of newly approved foreign companies. Of them, 555 cases, or 64.3 percent, took place in the service sector, up 17 percent from a year earlier.

Contributions—Over the past three decades, multinational companies have become deeply interwoven into China's economy and provided enormous momentum for its fast growth.

By the end of 2009, the Chinese Government had approved the establishment of 683,000 foreign-invested enterprises, said Zhang Xiaoqiang, Vice Chairman of the National Development and Reform Commission.

In 2009, foreign-invested enterprises provided 45 million jobs. Their industrial output accounted for 28 percent of the country's total, and taxes paid were about 22.7 percent of the country's total tax revenue that year, said Zhang. Foreign-invested enterprises are also China's major exporters and their exports accounted for 55.9 percent of the country's total in 2009.

In addition, multinationals have introduced modern industrial products and technologies into China and encouraged, through their examples, Chinese companies to restructure and practice modern corporate governance, said Wang.

Also, they helped cultivate a number of industries and accelerate China's industrialization process through technology transfers, and encouraged restructuring within the country's industrial sector through frequent cross-border M&As.

M&A will become a dominant investing strategy for multinationals in China. Thanks to these M&A activities, China's industries will grow bigger and more competitive, said Wang.

Multinationals also contributed to closer economic ties between China and their home countries, and easy access for China to international resources.

But they still face a number of challenges. While some multinationals have yet to find win-win solutions for themselves and China, others need to shoulder more social responsibilities, Wang said.

Notes:

1. **FDI（对外直接投资）:** Foreign direct investment (FDI) or foreign investment refers to long term participation by country A into country B. It usually involves participation in management, joint-venture, transfer of technology and expertise. There are two types of FDI: inward foreign direct investment and outward foreign direct investment, resulting in a *net* FDI *inflow* (positive or negative) and "stock of foreign direct investment", which is the cumulative number for a given period. Direct investment excludes investment through purchase of shares.

2. **MOFCOM（中华人民共和国商务部）**: MOFCOM (The Ministry of Commerce of the People's Republic of China, formerly Ministry of Foreign Trade and Economic Co-operation (对外贸易经济合作部，MOFTEC) is an executive agency of the State Council of China. It is responsible for formulating policy on foreign trade, export and import regulations, foreign direct investments, consumer protection, market competition and negotiating bilateral and multilateral trade agreements. The current Commerce minister is Chen Deming.

3. **Fortune 500（财富500强企业）**: The Fortune 500 is an annual list compiled and published by *Fortune* magazine that ranks the top 500 U. S. closely held and public corporations as ranked by their gross revenue after adjustments made by Fortune to exclude the impact of excise taxes companies collect. The list includes publicly and privately-held companies for which revenues are publicly available.

4. **National Development and Reform Commission（国家发展和改革委员会，缩写为 NDRC）**: The National Development and Reform Commission (NDRC), formerly State Planning Commission and State Development Planning Commission, is a macroeconomic management agency under the Chinese State Council, which has broad administrative and planning control over the Chinese economy. The NDRC's functions are to study and formulate policies for economic and social development, maintain the balance of economic development, and to guide restructuring of China's economic system. The NDRC has twenty-six functional departments/bureaus/offices with an authorized staff size of 890 civil servants.

Words & Expressions:

1. multinational [ˌmʌltiˈnæʃənəl] adj. 跨国公司的；多国的
   n. 跨国公司
2. relocate [ˌriːləʊˈkeit] vt. 重新安置；迁移
   vi. 重新安置；迁移新址
3. trailblazer [ˈtreilˌbleizə] n. 开拓者；开路的人；先驱者
4. milestone [ˈmailstəun] n. 里程碑，划时代的事件

5. logistics [ləu'dʒistiks] n. 后勤；后勤学
6. acquisition [ˌækwi'ziʃən] n. 收购
7. merger ['mə:dʒə] n. （企业等的）合并；并购；吸收（如刑法中重罪吸收轻罪）
8. interweave [ˌintə'wi:v] v. 互相编织
9. momentum [məu'mentəm] n. 势头；[物]动量；动力；冲力
10. restructure [ri:'strʌktʃə] vt. 调整；重建；更改结构
11. industrialization [inˌdʌstriəlai'zeiʃən] n. 工业化
12. governance ['gʌvənəns] n. 管理；统治；支配

Exercises:

I. Match the words on the left with their meanings on the right.

1. establishment   A. an organization created for business ventures
2. enterprise   B. someone who helps to open up a new line of research or technology or art
3. trailblazer   C. the act of transferring something from one form to another
4. merger   D. the combination of two or more commercial companies
5. interweave   E. an impelling force or strength
6. transfer   F. a public or private structure (business or governmental or educational) including buildings and equipment for business or residence
7. governance   G. handling an operation that involves providing labor and materials be supplied as needed
8. momentum   H. a branch of applied mathematics concerned with the collection and interpretation of quantitative data and the use of probability theory to estimate population parameters
9. statistics   I. interlace by or as it by weaving
10. logistics   J. the act of governing; exercising authority

II. Translate the following phrases into Chinese or English.

1. attract foreign investment
2. reform and opening up
3. a socialist market economy
4. product design
5. core raw materials
6. 技术服务部门
7. 区域经济学
8. 占……比例
9. 大举收购
10. 税收收入

III. Topic discussion.

1. Why does this report say that China remains the most popular destination for FDI?
2. What do you think are the main elements for the development of multinationals?
3. What do you think of mergers and acquisitions (M&As)?
4. What contributions do multinationals make to China?
5. How many famous multinationals do you know? What are they?

McDonald's Eyes Growing Presence in Local Market

SHANGHAI-A contemporary addition has joined Shanghai's traditional breakfast foods staples-McDonald's meals.

Since the corporation entered the Shanghai market in 1994, the popularity of the Egg McMuffin and its ilk is catching up to the city's longstanding morning meal favorites-dabing (Chinese pancakes), youtiao (deep-fried dough sticks), cifantuan (steamed sticky rice balls) and soymilk. And while this trend shows no sign of naturally slowing down, the multinational chain plans to step up efforts to accelerate it.

The fast food giant, headquartered in a suburb of Chicago-the city that hosts President Hu Jintao on Thursday-is trying to expand its China presence and adapt to the emerging power's ever-changing business environment.

"People in urban cities need a lot of convenience," McDonald's China CEO Kenneth Chan said.

"And everything has to be moderate in terms of how they spend their money, as everything is much more expensive in first-tier and second-tier cities."

McDonald's business model has been designed to meet such demand, Chan said. "We are located conveniently, open 24 hours with 24-hour delivery, and our breakfast starts at 5 am. Every day, we provide good value. And at the same time, we give our customers a break in a busy city life."

China, along with Australia and Japan, is one of the three biggest contributors to the company's business in the Asia-Pacific, Middle East and Africa regions. Having weathered SARS and the global recession, McDonald's has maintained double-digit annual growth nationwide, Chan said.

As the global foodservice leader, McDonald's plans to increase its investment in the country by 40 percent in 2011. It will open new restaurants, redesign old stores and introduce more convenient services, Chan said.

Between 175 and 200 new restaurants are projected to open across China in 2011. McDonald's will operate 2,000 restaurants in the country by 2013, Chan said. "It took 19 years to open 1,000 restaurants, and we are going to double that to 2,000," Chan said.

The chain currently operates about 1,300 stores in 150 cities across China, and its capital investment in the country has reached 7 billion yuan ($1.06 billion).

About 99 percent of McDonald's China's employees are Chinese, and the company is actively developing local talent to cultivate executives, Chan said.

In 2010, McDonald's spent 150 million yuan to open a Hamburger University in Shanghai. The school provides restaurant training for managers and executive classes to train future leaders.

In less than a year, Shanghai's Hamburger University has trained about 1,000 people, and at least 5,000 more graduates are expected in the next five years.

"If you want sustainable business you have to get local people to run the business," Chan said. "They know how to navigate in the business environment here, and they know the business status quo much better than somebody sitting in Chicago. We are getting close, and I am an Asian here."

Chan himself is also a beneficiary of McDonald's training. He joined the company as an assistant marketing manager in his native Singapore in 1993.

"At that time, I would not have imagined that one day I will be the managing director in Singapore," he said.

He came to the Chinese mainland in early 2009.

In addition to its retail business, McDonald's also has vast property investments.

Chan said the company is looking for more suitable locations, "especially those locations where we are able to put our drive-thru restaurants", Chan said.

Tips

Comparison of the World's 25 Largest Corporations with the GDP of Selected Countries (2010)

Company/Country	Revenues/GDP ($ billions)
Norway	414
South Africa	364
Greece	305
Exxon Mobil	285
Chevron	164
Romania	162
General Electric	157
Peru	154
Bank of America Corp.	150
ConocoPhilips	140
Ukraine	138
AT&T	123
Ford Motor	118
J. P. Morgan Chase & Co.	116
Hewlett-Packard	115
Berkshire Hathaway	112
Citigroup	109
Verizon Communications	108
McKesson	107
General Motors	105
Vietnam	104

续表

Company/Country	Revenues/GDP ($ billions)
American International Group	103
Bangladesh	100
Gardinal Heath	100
CVS Caremark	99
Wells Fargo	99
International Business Machines	96
United Health Group	87
Iraq	82
Procter & Gamble	80
Krpger	77
AmerisourceBergen	72
Costco Wholesale	71
Luxembourg	55

Sources: Fortune Magazine, May 2010 & World Bank, 2010.

Unit 6

Economic Regulations and Law

Text A U. S. Sets 21st Century Goal: Building a Better Patent Office

> 导读：20世纪，一项专利的申请书只有二十几页，十几条条款，但专利申请成功往往需要跌宕几年的时间。现在，随着计算机科学技术的发展及人类维权意识的提高，一项专利的申请书往往有好几十页，一百多条条款。因此，美国前总统奥巴马提出要使联邦专利与商标局实现现代化。联邦专利与商标局的现代化在专利申请的操作过程及范围上都对企业的产品发明的专利申请起着至关重要的作用。

WASHINGTON— President Obama, who emphasizes American innovation, says modernizing the federal Patent and Trademark Office is crucial to "winning the future." So at a time when a quarter of patent applications come from California, and many of those from Silicon Valley, the patent office is opening its first satellite office— in Detroit.

That is only one of the signs that have many critics saying that the office has its head firmly in the 20th century, if not the 19th.

Only in the last three years has the office begun to accept a majority of its applications in digital form. Mr. Obama astonished a group of technology executives last year when he described how the office has to print some applications filed by computer and scan them into another, incompatible computer system.

"There is no company I know of that would have permitted its information technology to get into the state we're in," David J. Kappos, who 18 months ago became director of the Patent and Trademark Office and undersecretary of commerce for intellectual property, said in a recent interview. "If it had, the CEO would have been fired, the board would have been thrown out, and you would have had shareholder lawsuits."

Once patent applications are in the system, they sit—for years. The patent office's pipeline is so clogged that it takes two years for an inventor to get an initial ruling, and an additional year or more before a patent is finally issued.

The delays and inefficiencies are more than a nuisance for inventors. Patentable ideas are the basis for many start-up companies and small businesses. Venture capitalists often require start-ups to have a patent before offering financing. That means that patent delays cost jobs, slow the economy and threaten the ability of American companies to compete with foreign businesses.

Much of the patent office's decline has occurred in the last 13 years, as the Internet age created a surge in applications. In 1997, 2.25 patents were pending for every one issued. By 2008, that rate had nearly tripled, to 6.6 patents pending for every one issued. The figure fell below six last year.

Though the office's ranks of patent examiners and its budget have increased by about 25 percent in the last five years, that has not been enough to keep up with a flood of applications—which grew to more than 2,000 a day last year, for a total of 509,000, from 950 a day in 1997.

The office, like a few other corners of the government, has long paid its way, thanks to application and maintenance fees. That income—$2.1 billion last year—has made it an inviting target for Congress, which over the last 20 years has diverted a total of $800 million to other uses, rather than letting the office invest the money in its operations.

Applications have also become far more complex, said Douglas K. Norman, president of the Intellectual Property Owners Association, a trade group mainly of large technology and manufacturing companies.

"When I was a young patent lawyer, a patent application would be 20 to 25 pages and have 10 to 15 claims," Mr. Norman said. A claim is the part of the patent that defines what is protected. "Now they run hundreds of pages, with hundreds, and sometimes thousands, of claims."

Lost in the scrutiny of the office's logjam, however, was the fact that the number of patents issued reached a record last year—more than 209,000, or 29 percent more than the average of 162,000 a year over the previous four years. Rejections also hit a high of 258,000—not a measure of quality, Mr. Kappos said, but a sign of greater efficiency.

Between the backlog of 700,000 patents awaiting their first action by an examiner and the 500,000 patents that are in process, a total of 1.2 million applications are pending.

Sitting in his suburban Virginia office, not far from a model of the light bulb Edison presented for patent in November 1879 (which was approved two and a half months later), Mr. Kappos proudly ticked off figures that he said proved the agency was heading in the right direction.

The backlog has actually declined about 10 percent from a peak of 770,000 at the end of 2008.

"We were able to work a 13-month year last year," he said, referring to the productivity increase in 2010 over the 2009. "We are processing a far larger workload with the same number of examiners."

Still, Mr. Kappos wants to add more than 1,000 examiners in each of the next two years, a 30 percent increase. Mr. Obama's 2012 budget calls for a 28 percent increase in spending, to $2.7 billion, over 2010. In two consecutive sessions, Congress has defeated a bill that would allow the patent office to keep all of the fees it collects. While another similar effort is under way, a big staffing increase will not be easy in a climate of cuts.

Mr. Kappos, a former electrical engineer and lawyer who joined the patent office in 2009 after 27 years at IBM, has improved relations with the union representing patent examiners. He and the union agreed on performance evaluation measures last year, the first time in 50 years that the yardsticks had been revised.

"I give David Kappos a good deal of credit for seeing where the problems have been and being willing to address them," said Robert D. Budens, president of the union, the Patent Office Professional Association. "I think it's a little early to see the full extent of the changes. But we have seen an increase in morale and a decrease in attrition, which is now almost the lowest it's been since I came here" in 1990.

Patent applications come from all over the United States, and the office has forgone satellite offices—until now. Last year, the office announced it would put about 100 examiners in Detroit. Some prominent lawmakers from Michigan have worked on patent issues, including Representative John Conyers Jr., a Detroit Democrat who, when the decision was made, was chairman of the House Judiciary Committee, which oversees patents.

Mr. Kappos said he chose Detroit because it had large communities of patent lawyers and agents, nearby universities and transportation centers, and relatively low costs of living and real estate. "Detroit has long been an innovation center," he said. "It's undervalued, and that is where we want to invest." He said it would also attract a work force with more varied skills.

Mr. Kappos is also pushing an initiative that would charge patent applicants a higher fee to guarantee that their applications will receive a ruling within a year. But that initiative and others are not enough, said Paul R. Michel, who recently retired as chief judge for the United States Court of Appeals for the Federal Circuit in Washington, the main forum for patent appeals.

"The office can't be made efficient in 18 months without a vast increase in finances," said Mr. Michel, who has made evangelizing for an overhaul of the office a pet cause. "Small efficiency improvements will only make a small difference in the problem."

Notes:

1. United States Patent and Trademark Office（美国专利商标局，缩写 PTO 或 USPTO）:
The United States Patent and Trademark Office (PTO or USPTO) is an agency in the United States Department of Commerce that issues patents to inventors and businesses for their inventions, and trademark registration for product and intellectual property identifica-tion.

The USPTO is based in Alexandria, Virginia, after a 2006 move from the Crystal City area of Arlington, Virginia. The offices under Patents and the Chief Information Officer that remained just outside the southern end of Crystal City completed moving to Randolph Square, a brand new building in Shirlington Village, on April 27, 2009. Since 1991, the office has been fully funded by fees charged for processing patents and trademarks. The head of the USPTO is David J. Kappos, who was sworn in on August 13, 2009 following the United States Senate's confirmation of his appointment by President Barack Obama. He succeeded John Doll, who served as acting head following the resignation of Jon W. Dudas at the end of the George W. Bush administration.

2. **Intellectual Property Owners Association**（知识产权所有者协会，缩写 **IPOA**）: The Intellectual Property Owners Association (IPO) is a trade association that is composed of owners of intellectual property (represented mostly by in-house corporate counsel and private practice attorneys practicing in the field) and other parties interested in intellectual property law. According to its "About IPO" page, the organization is composed about 200 companies and more than 10,000 individuals who are involved in the association either through their companies or as IPO inventor, author, executive, law firm or attorney members. IPO's corporate members file about 30 percent of the patent applications filed in the USPTO each year by U. S. nationals.

3. **Patent Office Professional Association**（美国专利局专业协会，缩写 **POPA**）: The Patent Office Professional Association (POPA) is a professional union of United States patent examiners（美国专利审查员）. It was formed in 1964.

4. **The House Judiciary Committee**（众议院司法委员会）: The U. S. House Committee on the Judiciary, also called the House Judiciary Committee, is a standing committee of the United States House of Representatives. It is charged with overseeing the administration of justice within the federal courts, administrative agencies and Federal law enforcement entities. The Judiciary Committee is also the committee responsible for impeachments of federal officials. Because of the legal nature of its oversight, committee

members usually have a legal background, but this is not required.

5. **The United States Courts of Appeals（美国上诉法院）**: The United States Courts of Appeals are considered among the most powerful and influential courts in the United States. Because of their ability to set legal precedent in regions that cover millions of people, the United States Courts of Appeals have strong policy influence on U. S. law; however, this political recognition is controversial. Moreover, because the U. S. Supreme Court chooses to hear fewer than 100 of the more than 10,000 cases filed with it annually, the United States Courts of Appeals serve as the final arbiter on most federal cases.

Words & Expressions:

1. astonish [əˈstɒnɪʃ] vt. 使惊讶
2. incompatible [ˌɪnkəmˈpætəbl] adj. 不相容的；矛盾的；不能同时成立的
3. undersecretary [ˌʌndəˈsekrətri] n. 副部长；次长
4. pipeline [ˈpaɪpˌlaɪn] n. 管道；输油管；传递途径
5. clog [klɒg] n. 障碍
6. nuisance [ˈnjuːsəns] n. 讨厌的人；【法律】妨害行为，骚扰行为，滋扰行为
7. surge [sɜːdʒ] n. 猛增；急剧上升
8. pend [pend] vt. 推迟对……的决定；使悬而不决
9. triple [ˈtrɪpl] vi. 增至三倍
10. maintenance [ˈmeɪntənəns] n. 维护，维修；保持；生活费用
11. divert [daɪˈvɜːt] vt. 转移；使……欢娱；使……转向
12. claim [kleɪm] n. 要求；声称；索赔；断言；值得
13. logjam [ˈlɒgdʒæm] n. 僵局；（河道等）受圆木阻塞；停滞状态；拥挤
14. backlog [ˈbæklɒg] n. [管理]积压的工作；积压待办的事务；大木材
15. workload [ˈwɜːkləʊd] n. 工作量
16. consecutive [kənˈsekjutɪv] adj. 连贯的；连续不断的

17. yardstick ['jɑːdstik] n. 衡量，评价的标准，尺度
18. morale [mɔˈrɑːl] n. 士气，精神面貌；民心；道德；品行
19. attrition [əˈtriʃən] n. 摩擦；磨损；消耗
20. forgo [fɔːˈɡəu] vt. 放弃；停止；对……断念
21. evangelize [iˈvændʒilaiz] vt. 传福音；使信基督教
22. overhaul [ˌəuvəˈhɔːl] vt. 分解检查，大修；追上并超过

Exercises:

I. Match the words on the left with their meanings on the right.

1. clog   A. work that a person is expected to do in a specified time
2. pending   B. any object that acts as a hindrance or obstruction
3. claim   C. do without or cease to hold or adhere to
4. logjam   D. awaiting conclusion or confirmation
5. workload   E. man-made equipment that orbits around the earth or the moon
6. incompatible F. an assertion of a right
7. forgo   G. any stoppage attributable to unusual activity
8. overhaul   H. examine hastily
9. scan   I. make repairs, renovations, revisions or adjustments to
10. satellite   J. not easy to combine harmoniously

II. Translate the following phrases into Chinese or English.

1. technology executives   2. intellectual property
3. patent applications   4. an initial ruling
5. start-up companies   6. 风险资本家
7. 提供融资   8. 生产率提高
9. 专利审查员   10. 绩效评估措施

III. Topic discussion.

1. How do you understand "winning the future" in Paragraphe One?
2. What consequences will patent delay make?
3. What do you think of patent? Do you think it is necessary?
4. What's the current situation of patent in your country?
5. What suggestions can you make to your government about the patent affairs?

Text B Anti-Trust Law Treats "All Firms Equally" over 140 Cases Handled: Rules in Line with International Principles

> 导读：2008年，中国政府阻止了可口可乐公司对国有品牌汇源果汁的收购案。因此，许多外国公司开始担心中国是否会利用反垄断法来不平等地对待国内与国外企业。但事实是中国在对待本国企业和外国企业的兼并收购时从来没有用过不同的评判标准，包括反垄断法的使用。在各类企业遵守市场规则的前提下，反垄断法始终是"公平对待每一家企业"。

BEIJING-China has "never discriminated" against foreign companies by using different standards in handling cases of mergers and acquisitions (M&A) involving the anti-trust law since its implementation in 2008, said a senior official of the Ministry of Commerce on Thursday.

Since the Chinese government blocked a proposed bid by Coca-Cola for China's top domestic juice maker Huiyuan at a price of $2.5 billion in 2008, there have been concerns that the country is unfairly treating foreign businesses by taking advantage of the anti-monopoly law.

The ministry said that, by the end of June, it had accepted and handled more than 140 M&A cases and approved 95 percent of them "with no strings attached".

STOP THE MERGERS! ENFORCE ANTI-TRUST LAWS!

"It's unreasonable to conclude that China discriminates or holds any bias against foreign firms by saying that we have banned or set restrictive requirements on some foreign cases," said Shang Ming, director-general of the ministry's anti-monopoly bureau.

The Coca-Cola bid was the only case turned down and five others were approved, although those came with additional restrictive requirements, according to the Ministry of Commerce.

All the six cases involved foreign companies.

He said the reason why China prohibited or set restrictive conditions on certain cases involving foreign firms is that "we found they owned a very high market share, and ... if approved, would exert negative impact on market competition".

The ministry said in April it had also started an anti-monopoly review on a merger proposal between mining giants BHP Billiton and Rio Tinto's iron ore joint venture.

China is the biggest buyer of iron ores. There were concerns that the merger of the two major mining companies would put its domestic steel industry at stake.

Organizations representing foreign companies such as the American Chamber of Commerce in China have said major State-owned companies should also be put under scrutiny in anti-trust approval, because many of them have a monopoly position.

Wu Hongwei, professor of law at Renmin University of China, said the accusations against China are groundless as the law is in line with international principles and are not discriminatory.

"No one can deny the progress China has made in opening its market just because of some complaints or pressures," he said.

The number of M&A applications presented to the ministry for approval will grow by 20 percent from a year earlier, as M&A cases worldwide are expected to pick up this year, Shang said.

The ministry said that, during the past two years, it has found a high ratio of foreign companies among the applicants for M&A approvals.

Under the Chinese anti-monopoly law, companies with annual turnovers of 10 billion yuan ($1.47 billion) globally and 400 million yuan in China, or combined turnovers of $2 billion in China, must get anti-trust approval for a proposed deal from the Chinese government.

Wei Xinghua, professor of economics with Renmin University of China, said that if an M&A deal is based on market rules, no objection should be raised. However, he said many foreign companies tried to monopolize sectors through the acquisition of local companies.

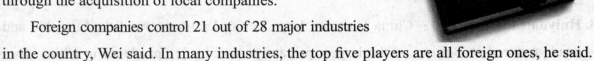

Foreign companies control 21 out of 28 major industries in the country, Wei said. In many industries, the top five players are all foreign ones, he said.

Shang said China will try to improve the anti-trust law by drafting some supplementary rules and regulations, as the law is still quite new in China. But the improvement will be made gradually, Shang said.

The anti-trust law took effect on Aug 1, 2008. A number of multinationals have been complaining about the slow pace and transparency of the evaluation and review process. In the case of Panasonic's takeover of Sanyo, the ministry accepted the filing four months after the company first lodged its file.

But Shang said the complaints "do not really make sense". Under the law, there are three phases in the review.

"Actually, in the review of majority of the cases, more than 60 percent was finished during the first phase and took less than 30 days. The rest took 90 days and even a few lasted 180 days," he said.

Notes:

1. **M&A（兼并和收购）**: The phrase mergers and acquisitions (abbreviated M&A) refers to the aspect of corporate strategy, corporate finance and management dealing with the buying, selling and combining of different companies that can aid, finance, or help a growing company in a given industry grow rapidly without having to create another business entity.

2. **Ministry of Commerce**（商务部）：The Ministry of Commerce People's Republic of China, formerly the Ministry of Foreign Trade and Economic Co-operation（对外贸易经济合作部，MOFTEC）is an executive agency of the State Council of China. It is responsible for formulating policy on foreign trade, export and import regulations, foreign direct investments, consumer protection, market competition and negotiating bilateral and multilateral trade agreements. The current Commerce minister is Chen Deming.

3. **Huiyuan**（汇源果汁）：China Huiyuan Juice Group Limited, established in 1992 and headquartered in Beijing, is the largest privately-owned juice producer in China. It is engaged in the manufacture and sales of juice and other beverage products. Its products include fruit juice and vegetable juice, nectars, bottled water, tea, and dairy drinks. It was listed on the Hong Kong Stock Exchange in 2007. In 3 September 2008, Atlantic Industries, the full subsidiary of Coca Cola Company agreed to buy China Huiyuan Juice for HK＄17.9 billion at HK＄12.20 per share, three times more than its closing price of HK＄4.14 on the previous day. Its shares closed at HK＄10.94 on that day. The proposed takeover was subject to anti-monopoly review by the Chinese Ministry of Commerce, which was scheduled to finish on 20 March 2009. On 17 March, it was reported that Coca Cola was considering abandoning the deal, as Chinese authorities insisted on relinquishing the Huiyuan brand name after acquisition. On 18 March, the Ministry of Commerce disallowed the bid, citing market competition concerns.

4. **BHP Billiton**（必和必拓公司）：BHP Billiton is a global mining and oil and gas company headquartered in Melbourne, Australia and with a major management office in London, United Kingdom. It is the world's largest mining company measured by revenues and, as of February 2011, the world's third-largest company measured by market capitalization. BHP Billiton was created in 2001 through the merger of the Australian Broken Hill Proprietary Company (BHP) and the Anglo-Dutch Billiton plc. The result is a dual-listed company. BHP Billiton Limited, which is the majority partner, has its primary listing on the Australian Securities Exchange and is the largest company in Australia measured by market capitalisation. BHP Billiton Plc has its primary listing on the London Stock

Exchange and is a constituent of the FTSE 100 Index.

5. **Rio Tinto（力拓集团）**: The Rio Tinto Group is a diversified, British-Australian, multinational mining and resources group with headquarters in London and Melbourne. The company was founded in 1873, when a multinational consortium of investors purchased a mine complex on the Rio Tinto River, in Huelva, Spain from the Spanish government. Since then, the company has grown through a long series of mergers and acquisitions to place itself among the world leaders in the production of many commodities, including aluminum, iron ore, copper, uranium, coal, and diamonds.

6. **Panasonic（松下电器）**: Panasonic Corporation, formerly known as Matsushita Electric Industrial Co., Ltd., is a Japanese multinational consumer Electronics Corporation headquartered in Kadoma, Osaka, Japan. Its main business is in electronics manufacturing and it produces products under a variety of names including Panasonic and Technics. Since its founding in 1918, it has grown to become the largest Japanese electronics producer. In addition to electronics, Panasonic offers non-electronic products and services such as home renovation services. Panasonic was ranked the 89th-largest company in the world in 2009 by the Forbes Global 2000 and is among the Worldwide Top 20 Semiconductor Sales Leaders.

7. **SANYO（三洋）**: SANYO Electric Co., Ltd. is a major electronics company and member of the Fortune 500 whose headquarters is located in Moriguchi, Osaka prefecture, Japan. Sanyo targets the middle of the market and has over 230 Subsidiaries and Affiliates. On December 21, 2009, Panasonic completed a 400 billion yen ($4.5 billion) acquisition of a 50.2% stake in Sanyo, making Sanyo a new subsidiary of Panasonic.

Words & Expressions:

1. anti-trust ['æntitrʌst] adj. 反垄断法；反托拉斯的
2. merger ['mə:dʒə] n. (企业等的)合并；并购；吸收
3. acquisition [,ækwi'ziʃən] n. 获得物，获得
4. implementation [,implimen'teiʃən] n.【法律】履行（契约等）
5. block [blɔk] vt. 阻止；阻塞；限制
6. anti-monopoly ['æntimə'nɔpəli] n. 反垄断
7. bias ['baiəs] n. 偏见；偏爱；
8. ban [bæn] vt. 禁止，取缔
9. restrictive [ri'striktiv] adj. 限制的；限制性的；约束的
10. bureau ['bjuərəu] (政府等机构的) 局；司；处；署，办公署
11. prohibit [prəu'hibit] vt. 阻止，禁止
12. exert [ig'zə:t] vt. 运用，发挥；施以影响
13. ore [ɔː] n. 矿；矿石
14. scrutiny ['skru:tini] n. 详细审查；监视；细看
15. accusation [,ækju:'zeiʃən] n. 控告，指控；谴责
16. ratio ['reiʃiəu] n. 比率，比例
17. applicant ['æplikənt] n. 申请人，申请者；请求者
18. transparency [træns'pærənsi] n. 透明，透明度
19. lodge [lɔdʒ] vt. 提出；寄存；借住；嵌入

Exercises:

I. Fill in the blanks with the suitable words given in the box. Change the form when necessary.

acquire	bid	propose	prohibit	exert
scrutiny	accuse	approve	implement	ratio

1. These could be adapted, he thinks, to provide effective _____ of managers.

2. Another _____ was to ban the use of primates caught in the wild.

3. Use of the drug has not declined since its _____.

4. She brazened through the _____ from the witness stand.

5. The census of 2000 and the CASS study both showed the _____ stable at around 120.

6. The draft legislation still requires parliamentary _____.

7. Yet even in the mature markets there could be consequences if a state fund is a big shareholder in a firm caught in a hostile _____.

8. The credit crunch has reduced merger and _____ (M&A) activity around the world.

9. _____ of authority over others is not always wise.

10. That is when bribery affects not just the _____ of policy, but its conception.

II. Translate the following phrases into Chinese or English.

1. market share
2. market competition
3. joint venture
4. at stake
5. state-owned companies
6. 联合营业额
7. 并购交易
8. 市场规则
9. 对……持有偏见
10. 反垄断法

III. Topic discussion.

1. What do you think of the monopoly phenomenon in your country?
2. Can you list some typical anti-trust cases?
3. How do you understand "with no strings attached" in Para. 3?
4. What influences will monopoly make on enterprises and customers?

5. Is there any efficient solution for the monopoly phenomenon?

Supplementary Reading

China E-Commerce Giant Launches Campaign to Fight Online Piracy

BEIJING-Taobao. com, China's leading B2C (business-to-consumer) website, announced on Monday that it will launch a major campaign to stop online piracy and counterfeiting. The move comes after the site was labeled as a "notorious market" by selling products that violate intellectual copyright protection.

The campaign, according to the website, will be joined by 89 international brands including LV, Gucci and Apple.

Last year, taobao.com deleted more than 5.7 million products involved in copyright infringement. However, while acknowledging the website's efforts, the Office of the United States Trade Representative was still not satisfied with the results.

In a February report entitled "Out-of-Cycle Review of Notorious Markets," the agency listed taobao. com as one of the online retailers that "exemplify key challenges in the global struggle against piracy and counterfeiting."

"Taobao's online copyright protection campaign will be launched regularly in the future. Once a case of selling pirated or counterfeited products is confirmed, we will immediately blacklist the seller and ban it from opening an outlet on the website," Qiao Beirui, a public relations principal with taobao. com, told Xinhua Monday.

According to Qiao, the website will also organize a special team responsible for checking piracy and counterfeiting.

In January, a group opposed to online piracy and counterfeiting, which was set up by more than 20 Internet companies, began operations.

The group has so far received more than 7,000 complaints, all of which occurred at taobao. com and involved more than 400 brands, according to group leader Huang Xiangru.

If left uncontrolled, counterfeit products and piracy on the Internet will severely harm the interests of hundreds of millions of online consumers and eventually damage the credibility of the Internet and the country, experts warned.

In this year's government work report, Premier Wen Jiabao said that the country would develop e-commerce, online shopping, geographical information and other new services in 2011.

Wen stressed that the government would go to greater lengths to crack down on intellectual copyright infringement and fake and shoddy products.

Urging quicker legislation in the field of e-commerce, many law experts noted that the country's current legislation and judicial regulations cannot be completely applied to online selling of pirated and shoddy products.

Lawyer Chen Baolong said that stronger supervision and management is of the greatest importance in order to root out online piracy.

"For taobao.com, they should conduct investigations and set up records for all online sellers, follow a register and checkup system and closely monitor the quality of products sold. On the other hand, the police should keep collecting evidence on online piracy each day and impose punishments on violators in a timely fashion," Chen said.

By the end of 2010, China had some 457 million internet users, the most in the world.

Figures from the China Internet Network Information Center show that 161 million Chinese citizens used the Internet to buy products last year, up 41.6 percent year on year.

Meanwhile, the China Internet Illegal Information Reporting Center received nearly 400,000 complaints last year, 23.8 percent of which pertained to online fraud.

In addition to efforts from the governments and sellers, customers were also advised to exercise caution in online shopping.

"If every consumer can remain clear-headed in front of the temptations of low-price international brands and be fully aware of intellectual copyright and self-protection, all the pirated and counterfeit products will have no way out—even in a virtual world," Chen said.

Tips

常用商法词汇：
- adhesion contract：定式合同，附从合同
- antitrust：反垄断
- bankruptcy：破产，倒闭

- blue laws：蓝法，指旧时禁止星期日营业、饮酒、娱乐等的规定
- civil law notarization：民法公证
- contracts：合同
- consideration：对价
- duress：威胁
- warranty：担保，保证
- breach of contract：违约，违反合同
- remedy：赔偿，补偿
- lien：扣押权，留置权
- juristic person：法人
- company (law)：公司法
- corporate law：企业法
- corporation：公司，法人（团体）
- incorporation (business)：公司，合并
- Delaware General Corporation Law (U. S.)：美国特拉华州普通公司法
- Limited liability company：股份有限公司
- fiduciary：信托
- partnership：合伙，合股
- agency：代理
- Escrow：暂交第三者保管的款项（或保证金、货物等）
- Trustee of a trust or executor of an estate; see also trusts and estates：信托和遗产
- charitable trust：慈善信托
- foundation：基金会
- association：协会
- cooperative：合作社
- class action：集团诉讼
- Cyber law：网络空间法
- Online Copyright Infringement Liability Limitation Act：网上著作权侵权限制法
- dispute resolution：调解纠纷
- alternative dispute resolution：替代性纠纷解决方式

- mediation：调解，仲裁，调停
- conciliation：调解
- negotiation：谈判
- arbitration：仲裁，调停
- binding arbitration：约束仲裁
- employment law：劳工法，雇佣法
- labor law：劳动法
- sexual harassment：性骚扰
- non-disclosure agreement：保密法
- estoppel：禁止翻供
- fraud deterrence：欺诈威慑
- industrial design rights：工业设计法
- intellectual property：知识产权
- Agreement on Trade-Related Aspects of Intellectual Property Rights (TRIPs)：与贸易有关的知识产权协定
- public domain：公共领域
- trade secret：商业机密
- patent：专利
- trademark：商标
- genericized trademark：商标
- People's Republic of China's Trademark Law：中华人民共和共商标法
- copyright：版权
- fair dealing：公平交易
- copyright infringement of software：软件版权侵犯
- list of copyright case law：版权法案例
- International trade law：国际贸易法
- law and economics：法律和经济
- land use：土地利用
- legal lexicography：法律词典编纂
- law dictionary：法律词典

- malpractice：渎职，利用职权营私舞弊
- notary public：公证人
- negotiable instruments：流通工具
- property law：财产法
- real property：不动产
- security interest：担保物权
- mechanics lien：机械扣押权
- product liability：产品责任权
- negligence：过失
- proximate cause：近因，直接原因
- mandatory labelling：强制性标签
- Racketeer Influenced and Corrupt Organizations Act：反诈骗腐败组织集团犯罪法
- release：放弃，让予（财产，权利等）
- tax law：税收法
- torts：侵权
- Uniform Commercial Code：统一商法
- Lex Mercatoria：商人法

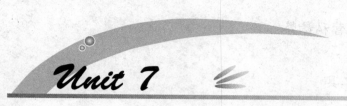

Unit 7

Human Resources Management

Text A Capturing the State of Human Resources in an Annual Report

> **导读**：人力资源管理是对组织内外相关人力资源进行有效开发、合理配置、充分利用和科学管理的制度、法令、程序和方法的总和。通过对人力资源的预测与规划，工作分析与设计，人力资源的维护与成本核算，人员的甄选录用、合理配置和使用，人员的智力开发、教育培训等过程，调动员工的工作积极性，发挥员工的潜能。定期的人力资源管理报告分析对公司诊断现状和预测未来情势大有裨益。

Sick-Leave pay cost the Arizona state government $907 per employee in 2002. Multiply that by 37,000 people on the state government's payroll, and the total comes to an unexpectedly high $33.5 million of the public's money. Those figures emerge from the Arizona Department of Administration's annual human resources report. It also highlights trends in sick-leave costs and helps the department initiate cost-saving measures, says the department's human resources director, Kathy Peckardt.

For instance, the report shows that sick leave cost $687 per employee five years earlier. This reflects a 32 percent hike over the five-year period between 1997 and 2002, or an amount equal to 3 percent of Arizona's current $1.2 billion payroll. "Agency directors are now taking steps to reduce unplanned absenteeism," Peckardt says. "The data in the annual report serves as a starting point to introduce wellness programs and target health care toward disease management and work/life programs. We hope to turn things around with the new initiatives."

At a time when human resources is redefining itself as a strategic business partner that is financially accountable for its programs and policies, an annual human resources report serves as a diagnostic and promotional tool. The regional governments, educational institutions and private corporations that produce these reports say that the data analysis sheds light on trends in the workforce, information that may not exist in monthly and quarterly summaries.

The municipality of Peel, in Ontario, Canada, has 3,500 employees who provide various services for its 1 million residents. Laura Nashman, commissioner of people, information and technology at the regional administrative body, is using a human resources report for the second year, and it has already saved her government about $300,000 (Canadian). "The report showed that we were spending hundreds of thousands on print ads that were not effective. Now, we have switched to a web-based system that costs a fraction of that," Nashman says. The cost savings form a significant part of her billion-dollar annual payroll.

Midwest Wireless in Mankato, Minnesota, has experimented with the report, and in the last year alone has saved more than $20,000 in the cost of hiring new people. "The metrics in our report persuaded managers that the employee-referral program was far more effective in leading to new hires than newspaper advertising, which they favored," says Lisa Jahnke, director of human resources at the firm. The 2004 report shows that of the 191 positions the company filled in 2003, 38 new hires came from employee referrals, compared to only four from newspaper advertising. Jahnke says that from now on, she will let the report do the talking. "We have it consistently documented, and so don't have to work on the persuading." The wireless company employs 590 people in 85 counties across Minnesota, Iowa and Wisconsin, and generated $214 million in revenue last year.

For both the large public organization and the small private company, the annual human resources report is a response to the evolving role of human-capital management. "Our employees self-serve through Web-based software," Jahnke says. "Our role is now more challenging. We have to add value to the bottom line, and be a proactive partner and illustrate how our activities link to the company's bottom line through cost-saving measures."

Nashman adds, "The annualized statistics on a variety of employment issues allow executives to base business planning on trend data. Simply providing monthly numbers without analysis is not valuable."

The human resources team at the Arizona Department of Administration has published an annual report for the past six years, as required by the state legislature. What began as a compilation of employee and payroll data is now a 34-page dossier focusing on employment trends, equal-opportunity information, employee mobility and results of employee feedback.

Midwest Wireless is in its second year with the report, and Jahnke is its chief architect. "Consider HR like any business, and a business must have an annual report. We make every person in the department list their own goals and accomplishments during the year. It was painful at first, but we now have greater accountability within the department."

The Region of Peel has a 33-page document that looks at staffing and benefits statistics and includes a discussion of a topical human resources issue. "In providing the information just once a year, we find that more people actually read it," Nashman says. "It is more thought provoking, as it focuses on trends rather than statistics at a point in time."

The annual reports target decision-makers in an organization. Peckardt says that two members of her team take up to 60 days to piece together the data before presenting it to the governor and legislature. The report is then posted on the Internet, Peckardt says, and private corporations use the data to determine their own salary benchmarks and benefit packages.

Jahnke says that the 60-page document is looked at by C-level executives and takes 70 man-hours to put together. "The first report was much more excruciating, as the company was not accustomed to collecting data in the format. The second time around, we were able to take actionable steps as a result of the data contained in the report. We reduced time to hire and cost of hiring by using strategies that work better for us. Next year, we are focusing on linking activities of HR to the company's bottom line, through the budget and more cost-saving measures," Jahnke says. Her current annual report details strengths and weaknesses of the organization, hiring costs and results, training and development usage, and initiatives for the year.

Despite the time and personnel costs that go into preparing such a document, advocates say the reports are a good promotional tool for the human resources department. "The annual report is a quick reference tool that provides information in a very user-friendly format. In fact, it serves as a time-saving measure, as we do not have to repeatedly gather data," Peckardt says. "For us, it doubles up as an excellent tool to have information at our fingertips for the media and members of the public."

More important, the reports have a direct positive impact on each organization's bottom line through introducing cost-saving measures. The annual reports also point to systemic weaknesses. The Arizona annual report shows that the state's workforce has shrunk by 2,000 employees because state pay lags behind market salaries in the private sector by 16.3 percent. Peckardt says that budget negotiations currently under way in the state legislature include a plan to raise government pay by up to $1,000 per employee, or by 2 percent.

While annual reports have produced tangible results for these organizations, only a handful of other players generate them. They include Dartmouth College, University of Saskatchewan and University of Texas Medical Branch. Others, like Minnesota-based Fairview Health Services, tried producing a formalized annual report but dropped it. Yet others, such as Intel Corp., opt for less sophisticated informal annual reviews. "Our year-end review is simply an E-mail document that provides a progress report: what was achieved, what was missed, a summary of the year and perhaps a view to what's anticipated," says company spokesperson Gail Dundas.

Consultants say that most in the private sector are not impressed by the annual report's utility. "Our experience with clients has been that it is often companies that perceive problems in the workforce who use such a report," says Rob Landau, benefits attorney with the Hay Group in Arlington, Virginia. "Also, such reports are used more often by companies where the HR information system is preprogrammed to readily produce one." Even in cases where the system lends itself to regular metrics, Landau says, managers often demand data on the workforce on a quarterly basis.

Landau does confirm the report's effectiveness as a prognostic tool. "The annual report grows out of the Sarbanes-Oxley movement to transparency and accountability and is more widespread in government organizations," he says. "Undoubtedly, there is an advantage to having all the information in one place for everyone to reach for on his or her bookshelves. But as HR departments continue to be downsized, consultants may be better placed to take on projects like this."

SAS Institute sells an information-management tool to 100 clients worldwide to assist in generating periodic reports based on human-capital metrics. Daniel Minto, director of human capital management solutions, says that strategic decisions cannot be based on short-term monthly or quarterly data. "The annual report draws out subtle trends in the organization."

Advocates of the report stress that monthly and quarterly reviews don't provide the sense of perspective that an annual report does. "Some employee surveys are only feasible on an annual basis. Also, our sick-leave trend is troubling, but we only noticed it when we had the year's data to look at," Nashman says. Minto says that data used to be provided on a transaction basis. "Now, across HR, we are seeing a movement toward a trend-analysis mind-set as our clients see the value of data on an annualized basis and are demanding more of it."

Notes:

1. **Human Resources（人力资源，缩写 HR）:** Human resources is a term used to describe the individuals who comprise the workforce of an organization. It is also the name of the function within an organization charged with the overall responsibility for implementing strategies and policies relating to the management of individuals. Human resources is a relatively modern management term, coined in the 1960s. The origins of the function arose in organizations that introduced 'welfare management' practices and also in those that

adopted the principles of "scientific management". From these terms emerged a largely administrative management activity, co-ordinating a range of worker related processes and becoming known, in time as the 'personnel function'. Human resources progressively became the more usual name for this function, in the first instance in the United States as well as multinational corporations, reflecting the adoption of a more quantitative as well as strategic approach to workforce management, demanded by corporate management and the greater competitiveness for limited and highly skilled workers.

2. **The Regional Municipality of Peel（also known as Peel Region，加拿大皮尔区）**: a regional municipality in Southern Ontario, Canada. It consists of three municipalities to the west and northwest of Toronto: the cities of Brampton and Mississauga, and the town of Caledon. The entire region is part of the Greater Toronto Area and the inner ring of Golden Horseshoe. The regional seat is in Brampton. With a population of 1,159,405 (2006 census), Peel Region is the second-largest municipality in Ontario after Toronto. Owing to immigration and its transportation infrastructure (with seven 400-series highways serving the region, and Toronto Pearson International Airport located mostly within its boundaries), Peel Region is a rapidly-growing area with a young population and an increasing profile.

3. **C-Level Executives（C级管理人员）**: The highest level executives are usually called "C-level" or part of the "C-suite", referring to the 3-letter initials starting with "C" and ending with "O" (for "Chief _____ Officer"); the major traditional such offices are Chief Executive Officer (CEO), Chief Operations Officer (COO), and Chief Financial Officer (CFO). In technology companies, a Chief Technology Officer (CTO) is also central, and for companies with a strong IT capacity a Chief Information Officer (CIO) is also significant. (Most other C-level titles are not universally recognized, and tend to be specific to particular organizational cultures or preferences.)

Words & Expressions:

1. multiply ['mʌltiplai] vt. 乘；使增加；使繁殖；使相乘
   vi. 乘；繁殖；增加
   adv. 多样地；复合地
   adj. 多层的；多样的
2. highlight ['hailait] vt. 突出；强调；使显著；加亮
   n. 最精彩的部分；最重要的事情；加亮区
3. initiate [i'niʃieit] vt. 开始，创始；发起；使初步了解
   n. 开始；新加入者，接受初步知识者
   adj. 新加入的；接受初步知识的
4. absenteeism [,æbsən'ti:izəm] n. 旷工；旷课；有计划的怠工；经常无故缺席
5. diagnostic [,daiəg'nɔstik] adj. 诊断的；特征的
   n. 诊断法；诊断结论
6. shed [ʃed] vt. 流出；摆脱；散发；倾吐
   vi. 流出；脱落；散布
   n. 小屋，棚；分水岭
7. municipality [mju:,nisi'pæləti] n. 市民；市政当局；自治市或区
8. metric ['metrik] adj. 公制的；米制的；公尺的
   n. 度量标准
9. referral [ri'fə:rəl] n. 参照；提及；被推举的人；转诊病人
10. evolving [i'vɔlv] adj. 进化的；展开的
11. proactive [,prəu'æktiv] adj. 前摄的（前一活动中的因素对后一活动造成影响的）；有前瞻性的，先行一步的
12. illustrate ['iləstreit] vt. 阐明，举例说明；图解
    vi. 举例
13. legislature ['ledʒisleitʃə] n. 立法机关；立法机构
14. compilation [,kɔmpi'leiʃən] n. 编辑
15. dossier ['dɔsiei,dəu'sjei] n. 档案，卷宗；病历表册

16. provoke [prəu'vəuk] vt. 驱使；激怒；煽动；惹起
17. benchmark ['bentʃmɑːk] n. 基准；标准检查程序
    vt. 用基准问题测试（计算机系统等）
18. excruciate [ik'skruːʃieit] vt. 使苦恼；施酷刑；折磨
19. tangible ['tændʒəbl] adj. 有形的；切实的；可触摸的
    n. 有形资产
20. prognostic [prɔg'nɔstik] n. 预兆；预言；预后症状
    adj. 预后的；预兆的
21. transparency [træns'pærənsi] n. 透明，透明度；幻灯片；有图案的玻璃
22. feasible ['fiːzəbl] adj. 可行的；可能的；可实行的
23. transaction [træn'zækʃən] n. 交易；事务；办理；会报，学报

Exercises:

I. **Fill in the blanks with the suitable words given in the box. Change the form when necessary.**

illustrate	compilation	tangible	proactive	transaction
provoke	highlight	transparency	municipality	diagnostic

1. E-government is no magic bullet, but it gives citizens and lobby groups more power to scrutinize government and _____ waste and dishonesty.

2. There is some hope that in the near future this simple and relatively safe assay may become routine in viral _____ laboratories.

3. The comprehensive plan for a _____ directly under the Central Government shall be submitted by the people's government of the _____ to the State Council for examination and approval.

4. China will continue to implement the _____ fiscal policy and the prudent monetary policy, and simultaneously adopt other necessary macroeconomic policies.

5. A single example will serve to _____ the point.

6. Any _____ becomes outdated nearly as soon as it is printed.

7. Such tendentious statements are likely to _____ strong opposition.

8. For those who do invest their savings it would normally be in the form of something _____.

9. A machine for projecting the images of opaque objects or _____ on a screen.

10. His failure in this _____ was due to nothing else than his own carelessness.

Ⅱ. **Decide whether the following statements are true (T) or false (F) according to the passage.**

1. The report showed that the expenditure of hundreds of thousands on print ads was worthing and effective. (   )

2. Because the annual sick-leave pay cost is too high, so now the government has switched to a Web-based system that costs a fraction of that. (   )

3. The 2004 report showed that of all the positions the company filled in 2003, many hires came from employee referrals, exceeding a lot to those from newspaper advertising. (   )

4. Strategic decisions can be accorded to short-term monthly or quarterly data. (   )

5. Only on an annual basis, some employee surveys are workable. (   )

Ⅲ. **Translate the following sentences into Chinese.**

1. For instance, the report shows that sick leave cost $687 per employee five years earlier. This reflects a 32 percent hike over the five-year period between 1997 and 2002, or an amount equal to 3 percent of Arizona's current $1.2 billion payroll.

2. At a time when human resources is redefining itself as a strategic business partner that is financially accountable for its programs and policies, an annual human resources report serves as a diagnostic and promotional tool.

3. We have to add value to the bottom line, and be a proactive partner and illustrate how our activities link to the company's bottom line through cost-saving measures.

4. What began as a compilation of employee and payroll data is now a 34-page dossier focusing on employment trends, equal-opportunity information, employee mobility

and results of employee feedback.

5. Undoubtedly, there is an advantage to having all the information in one place for everyone to reach for on his or her bookshelves. But as HR departments continue to be downsized, consultants may be better placed to take on projects like this.

Text B The Tech Effect on Human Resources

> **导读**：人力资源管理，是在经济学与人本思想指导下，通过招聘、甄选、培训、报酬等管理形式对组织内外相关人力资源进行有效运用，满足组织当前及未来发展的需要，保证组织目标实现与成员发展的最大化。它是预测组织人力资源需求并做出人力需求计划、招聘选择人员并进行有效组织、考核绩效支付报酬并进行有效激励、结合组织与个人需要进行有效开发以便实现最优组织绩效的全过程。21世纪是全球化、市场化、信息化的世纪，是知识主宰的世纪。在新经济条件下，企业人力资源管理必然要发生相应的变化。因此，企业人力资源管理系统将构筑在Internet/Intranet 的计算机网络平台上，形成新型的人力资源管理模式。

Today, core HR responsibilities as diverse as recruitment, oversight of legal and regulatory compliance, benefits administration, and the safeguarding of confidential employee information cannot be carried out effectively without high-tech tools.

In a world where what matters gets measured, many HR executives are turning to sophisticated analytics to gauge their department's strategic contributions. In addition, many HR managers are borrowing from other business disciplines and integrating collaborative and social networking tools such as listservs, Facebook applications and video.

For these HR professionals, the growth of electronic communication and Internet use requires developing policies governing the safekeeping and appropriate flow of information, including E-mails and blogs. Indeed HR professionals, working in tandem with information technologists, now rely on policy and software to monitor data flow, block inappropriate data such as pornography, and prevent the leaking of trade secrets.

HR professionals also rely on automated systems to direct employee benefit contributions. Such systems automatically direct a portion of workers "pay toward their retirement" savings plans unless employees opt out, for instance.

And while total rewards statements that alert employees to the total value of their compensation benefits packages have been around for years, many companies now are making that information available to workers electronically through HR information systems or self-service sites.

Workplace diversity initiatives are getting a boost from technology. Remarkable developments in assistive technology, for example, have increased job opportunities for people with physical disabilities. Some employers say that investing in such technologies is simply the right thing to do; others argue that such initiatives are good for the bottom line since they allow companies to recruit from a broader pool.

Employers are also turning to technology to assist in evaluating their workers and vice versa. Electronic systems can automate performance-management processes, ensure an accurate "grading curve" and guarantee feedback to employees.

Meanwhile, many companies are relying on technology to streamline traditionally cumbersome employee surveys.

Technology has significant impact on organization and employee development in such areas as e-learning, computer-based testing and workplace collaboration. Organizations are increasingly using technology in training.

Human resources professionals are upping their reliance on technology to manage safety and security information and functions. Workplace safety and security can benefit from technology by facilitating acquisition and analysis of injury and illness data, injury costs per employee, training documentation and management, performance management, electronic communications, digital access key log-in information, security camera data management and identity theft protection.

Biometrics devices that use fingerprints or other physical traits for identification can help solve some employee discipline problems and protect sensitive data. Time clocks are one of a growing number of workplace applications of biometrics.

During the last decade, the Internet has played a growing role in external recruiting. Large, all-purpose online job boards quickly found a place in recruitment. Meanwhile, niche sites catering to specific industries and demographic niches such as women and Asians won favor. Online corporate job sites and intranets have become key recruiting tools, allowing employers to get the word out about job openings quickly and inexpensively.

Employers also are using technology to market job openings more strategically. Many capitalize on emerging technology like RSS—real simple syndication— allowing online postings to reach job seekers via E-mail or text message as soon as a new job is posted. Others are enhancing traditional online listings with videos and podcasts.

Meanwhile, employers have had to adapt to tech-savvy candidates and multimedia resumes that include text, photos, video and sound.

Technology is also playing a pivotal role in the controversy regarding illegal immigration. Tens of thousands of employers are voluntarily using e-Verify, an Internet-powered tool offered free by the Social Security Administration and the U. S. Department of Homeland Security, to verify a match between employees' names, Social Security numbers and immigration information.

Once an application comes in, many HR professionals tap desktop search engines such as Google to check backgrounds. A few employers check out workers' private blogs and entries they may have placed on social networking sites such as Facebook and MySpace. Others sign up for help from computerized background screening services.

And once a new hire comes on board, many HR professionals are relying on electronic onboarding systems to handle tasks including assigning parking passes, computers, uniforms, E-mail addresses and security badges. Some employers—particularly those with a scattered workforce—are capitalizing on computerized learning systems for orientation and to deliver coaching on topics from sexual harassment avoidance to conflict resolution.

Notes:

1. **Grading Curve**（级配曲线测量法）: In education, grading on a curve (also known as curved grading or simply curving) is a statistical method of assigning grades designed to yield a predetermined distribution of grades among the students in a class. The term "curve" refers to the "bell curve", the graphical representation of the probability density of the normal distribution (also called the Gaussian distribution), but this method of grading does not necessarily make use of any specific frequency distribution such as the bellshaped normal distribution. One method of applying a curve uses these three steps: First, numeric scores (or possibly scores on a sufficiently finegrained ordinal scale) are assigned to the students. The actual values are unimportant as long as the ordering of the scores corresponds to the ordering of how good the students are. In the second step these scores are converted to percentiles (or some other system of quantiles). Finally, the percentile values are transformed to grades according to a division of the percentile scale into intervals, where the interval width of each grade indicates the desired relative frequency for that grade.

2. **E-learning**（网络学习）: E-learning comprises all forms of electronically supported learning and teaching. The information and communication systems, whether networked or not, serve as specific media to implement the learning process. The term will still most likely be utilized to reference out-of-classroom and in-classroom educational experiences via technology, even as advances continue in regard to devices and curriculum. E-learning is essentially the computer and network-enabled transfer of skills and knowledge. E-learning applications and processes include web-based learning, computer-based learning, virtual classroom opportunities and digital collaboration. Content is delivered via the Internet, intranet/extranet, audio or video tape, satellite TV, and CD-ROM. It can be self-paced or instructor-led and includes media in the form of text, image, animation, streaming video and audio.

3. **Computer-Based Testing（电脑化测验）**: A Computer-Based Assessment (CBA), also known as Computer-Based Testing (CBT), e-assessment, computerized testing and computer-administered testing, is a method of administering tests in which the responses are electronically recorded, assessed, or both. As the name implies, Computer-Based Assessment makes use of a computer or an equivalent electronic device such as a cell phone or PDA. CBA systems enable educators and trainers to author, schedule, deliver, and report on surveys, quizzes, tests and exams. Computer-Based Assessment may be a standalone system or a part of a virtual learning environment, possibly accessed via the World Wide Web.

4. **RSS（简易信息聚合，Really Simple Syndication）**: RSS (most commonly expanded as Really Simple Syndication) is a family of web feed formats used to publish frequently updated works—such as blog entries, news headlines, audio, and video—in a standardized format. An RSS document (which is called a "feed", "web feed", or "channel") includes full or summarized text, plus metadata such as publishing dates and authorship. Web feeds benefit publishers by letting them syndicate content automatically. They benefit readers who want to subscribe to timely updates from favored websites or to aggregate feeds from many sites into one place. RSS feeds can be read using software called an "RSS reader", "feed reader", or "aggregator", which can be web-based, desktop-based, or mobile-device-based. A standardized XML file format allows the information to be published once and viewed by many different programs. The user subscribes to a feed by entering into the reader the feed's URI or by clicking a feed icon in a web browser that initiates the subscription process. The RSS reader checks the user's subscribed feeds regularly for new work, downloads any updates that it finds, and provides a user interface to monitor and read the feeds. RSS allows users to avoid manually inspecting all of the websites they are interested in, and instead subscribe to websites such that all new content is pushed onto their browsers when it becomes available.

Words & Expressions:

1. recruitment [ri'kru:tmənt] n. 招聘；补充；征募新兵
2. oversight ['əuvəsait] n. 监督，照管；疏忽
3. compliance [kəm'plaiəns] n. 顺从，服从；承诺
4. sophisticate [sə'fistikeit] vt. 弄复杂；使变得世故；曲解
   n. 久经世故的人；精通者
   vi. 诡辩
5. gauge [geidʒ] n. 计量器；标准尺寸；容量规格
   vt. 测量；估计；给……定规格
6. collaborative [kə'læbərətiv] adj. 合作的，协作的
7. tandem ['tændəm] n. 串联；串座双人自行车
   adj. 串联的
   adv. 一前一后地；纵排地
8. opt out 决定退出；插播；请求免除
9. compensation [,kɔmpen'seiʃən] n. 补偿；报酬；赔偿金
10. boost [bu:st] vt. 促进；增加；支援
    vi. 宣扬；偷窃
    n. 推动；帮助；宣扬
11. vice versa [,vaisi'və:sə] 反之亦然
12. accurate ['ækjurət] adj. 精确的
13. streamline ['stri:mlain] vt. 使合理化；使成流线型
    n. 流线；流线型
    adj. 流线型的
14. cumbersome ['kʌmbəsəm] adj. 笨重的；累赘的；难处理的
15. biometric [,baiəu'metrik] adj. 生物计量的 n. 计量生物学
16. niche [ni:ʃ,nitʃ] n. 壁龛；合适的职业
    vt. 放入壁龛
17. cater ['keitə] vt. 投合，迎合；满足需要；提供饮食及服务
18. capitalize ['kæpitəlaiz] vt. 使资本化；以大写字母写；估计……的价值
    vi. 利用；积累资本

19. enhance [ɪnˈhɑːns] vt. 提高；加强；增加
20. podcast [ˈpɒdkʌst] n. 播客
21. savvy [ˈsævi] n. 悟性；理解能力 vt. 理解；懂
    　　　　　　　　　　　vi. 理解；知道
22. pivotal [ˈpɪvətl] adj. 关键的；中枢的；枢轴的
    　　　　　　　　　 n. 关键事物；中心事物
23. controversy [ˈkɒntrəˌvɜːsi] n. 争论；论战；辩论；理解；知道
24. scatter [ˈskætə] vi. 分散，散开；散射
    　　　　　　　　 vt. 使散射；使散开；使分散；使散播，使撒播
    　　　　　　　　 n. 分散；散播，撒播
25. harassment [ˈhærəsmənt] n. 骚扰；烦恼

Exercises:

I. Match the words on the left with their meanings on the right.

1. recruitment　　　A. acting according to certain accepted standards
2. oversight　　　　B. something (such as money) given or received as payment or reparation (as for a service or loss or injury)
3. compliance　　　C. a feeling of intense annoyance caused by being tormented
4. compensation　　D. difficult to handle or use especially because of size or weight
5. boost　　　　　　E. the cognitive condition of someone who understands
6. streamline　　　F. a dispute where there is strong disagreement
7. cumbersome　　　G. an unintentional omission resulting from failure to notice something
8. savvy　　　　　　H. the act of giving hope or support to someone
9. controversy　　　I. the act of getting recruits; enlisting people for the army (or for a job or a cause etc.)
10. harassment　　　J. contour economically or efficiently

II. Read the following text and fill in the blanks with the words given on the box.

| advertise | persuade | according | basis | superior |
| compete | outfit | budget | appeal | measurable |

As Laura Martin, an analyst at Needham & Company, an investment bank, observes, the internet now (1) _____ fiercely for the kind of (2) _____ that is carried on the radio, in newspapers and in many magazines. Campaigns to (3) _____ people to consider one product over another, or actually to go out and buy something, are well-suited to digital (4) _____, with their (5) _____ ability to track and segment audiences. Mobile ad platforms know where people are. Google can hit customers when they seem to show an interest in products. Such marketing is also (6) _____, which (7) _____ to firms when (8) _____ are tight. In the past four years the share of American online advertising spending that is bought on the (9) _____ of performance has risen from 41% to 59%, (10) _____ to the Interactive Advertising Bureau.

Supplementary Reading

Risk Management and Human Resources Team up to Cut Absence Costs

While pregnant with her first child in 1997, Tricia Chambers was diagnosed with breast cancer. "My six-week maternity leave turned into a yearlong absence," she says. But as manager of occupational health and risk for Osram Sylvania, the $2 billion lighting manufacturing company based in Danvers, Massachusetts, she couldn't stay away that long. To minimize the impact, Chambers, now cancer-free, telecommuted and went to an abbreviated schedule before returning full-time.

The year before, her colleague Christine Sheedy, Osram Sylvania's risk manager, had complications after childbirth and was out for 12 weeks instead of 6. Then, in 2003, her youngest son was hit by a car. He's fine now, but Sheedy used up a week of family medical leave to help care for him.

The duo's personal experiences with disability, while difficult, have made them more efficient, insightful and empathetic as the brains behind Osram Sylvania's new integrated disability-management program. These days, they are often asked to speak at industry conferences, and their program is being held up as a model.

And for good reasons. In one year's time, the company shrank $5 million in annual short-term disability costs to $4.2 million for its 9,000 U.S. employees. The program has saved 25 percent in direct costs in the first year and is projected to cut costs by up to half in its first three years.

"In the first year, the average time off went from 48 days to 38," Chambers says. "We estimate that for our company, for every day we can reduce duration, it's $100,000 in savings."

The personal experiences of Chambers and Sheedy lend credibility to their efforts. When employees who are running out of medical leave or are in some other crisis mode complain that no one understands, they can say, "Oh yes, we do." Their empathy partially explains the success, they contend. "When employees are using this program, they are usually in some stage of crisis," Chambers says. "We try to keep this in mind."

"Integrated disability management is a term that's been infiltrating business for the past decade, and in the process it is changing operations and bottom lines, says Karen Trumbull English, a partner at Spring Consulting Group, a Boston-based firm that provides consulting services and helped Osram Sylvania with its new program.

While there are different terms to describe the new approach—integrated disability management, total absence management, health and productivity management—the concept is the same. Companies are managing occupational and off-the-job absences under a single umbrella and focusing on the fact that non-occupational absences are manageable, no matter what conventional wisdom says.

The larger the company, the more likely it is to have an integrated disability-management program, says Shelly Wolff, national practice leader for health and productivity for Watson Wyatt Worldwide in Stamford, Connecticut. Among the 120 employers with more than 5,000 workers surveyed last year by Watson Wyatt, about half have integrated programs, Wolff says.

The story of Osram Sylvania's new integrated disability-management program began almost two years ago, when the company faced a costly, complex problem shared by many U.S. companies. Disability claims were increasing, and the impact of these costs was becoming more dramatic. The company's processes for managing them were becoming inadequate, say Chambers and Sheedy.

The other problem: the disability-management and workers' compensation systems were not linked, and that resulted in inconsistent policies and procedures as well as duplicated costs and inefficiency. As a result of the disjointed systems, an employee injured on the job was treated differently from a worker injured on personal time, even if the illness or injury was identical.

The challenges that Sheedy and Chambers faced are familiar to many of their colleagues. Says Sheedy: "Disability management is one of the most problematic areas for companies today, made even more glaring by pressures to hold down costs, boost productivity and provide opportunity for disabled employees to return to work." And losses are even greater at companies that don't have integrated disability-management systems in place.

Their goal, in the face of that challenge, was to make the handling of all leaves effective, equitable and efficient, whether they were granted for workers' compensation, disability or FMLA. As a model, they looked to their recently completed overhaul of Osram Sylvania's workers' compensation program. "In an eight-year period," says Chambers, "we reduced claims by 35 percent and shaved $10 million in losses from the program." The success of that program, they say, resulted from their focus on three challenges: keeping workers productive and at work, returning them promptly to the job and coordinating multiple vendors, payment processes and claims-payment strategies.

They instituted a medical-case-management program that encourages workers to quickly report injuries, works with them to develop treatment plans and refers them to health-care providers that can aid in early return to work. They hired a legal specialist at headquarters to oversee claims at each of the company's 22 manufacturing locations and placed occupational-health-risk nurse specialists at 18 of the biggest locations. They put in a new allocation system that charged each location for losses and reduced medical costs by establishing a managed-care arrangement, which was the more economical option, whenever possible.

"When we saw success there, on the occupational side," says Chambers, "we asked management to manage the non-occupational cases, including short-term and long-term disability and the Family and Medical Leave Act." It is unusual for the human resources and risk management departments to team up, Chambers and Sheedy acknowledge. "The HR side is more used to dealing face-to-face with an employee," Chambers says. "On the risk side, there is less of that and more number-crunching."

Their first step was to quantify the direct costs of absences, which meant pulling data from payroll, vendor-claims databases and other sources, and then verifying it. They added in indirect costs, an elusive and sometimes unattainable number. They investigated, for instance, whether temporary employees are hired to cover for absent ones, whether benefits continue to be paid during the absence and whether overtime increases to make up for the absent employee. They looked at factors driving up the direct costs of absences, such as increased litigation or insufficient return-to-work accommodations, which would include a shorter work schedule and telecommuting options.

They also found that some conventional wisdom about non-occupational costs was incorrect.

"Everyone assumes that worker's comp costs are more than non-occupational disability costs," Chambers says. But she and Sheedy had a gut feeling that this isn't always the case, and they were right. At Osram, the non-occupational costs, at $5 million annually, were two times higher than the occupational costs.

Once they had identified the potential cost-savings, the two launched a program that focuses on timely reporting of illness and injury, aggressive medical and case management, consistent tracking of leaves, timely return to work and accommodation, so the job can be modified to ease a worker's return.

The primary goal was to have absences managed consistently, whether they were due to on-the-job or off-the-job injuries or ailments. "What wasn't right was that absences were handled inconsistently," Sheedy says. "We were working to manage workers' comp in a certain way, and for non-occupational work or injury, the process was different."

The medical approaches were very different as well, adds Chambers. "On the non-occupational side, we had less control over primary healthcare providers."

So treating absences the same, whatever their cause, was the primary goal. But along the way, a number of other goals emerged. For instance, they integrated the occupational-absence system's  best practices into the non-occupational-absence system, which includes short-and long-term disability and family medical leave.

Calling the program "integrated" isn't quite correct, says Chambers. "Coordinated" is a better description. "Under integrated, all data systems are funneled through one vendor," she says. But that's often not feasible. "We coordinate multiple vendors on one project or overall philosophy."

The overhaul of non-occupational absence required an attitude shift among employees and supervisors, Chambers and Sheedy found. It meant that workers had to move from feeling entitled to absences to understanding that it was their responsibility to manage them. They had to shift from a focus on disability to a focus on returning to work. The company would have to make them feel accountable for their time away from work as well. For its part, the company had to change its fragmented view of disability.

"Historically, most companies saw the occupational injuries and illnesses as their responsibility and something to financially manage," Chambers says. "And the non-occupational side of disability benefits was non-manageable." But given rising health-care costs, "we are looking at disability as a whole, not just looking at whose liability it is."

"We need to focus on the disability and what the employee can do, not what he or she can't do," Chambers says. "It's a mental shift and an extreme culture change. We had resistance in the beginning. Employees felt we have no right to meddle."

To overcome the grumbling about that involvement, "we focused on fairness to all employees," Chambers says. In many meetings, she and Sheedy explained the new concept from that fairness perspective. They issued general corporate announcements to let workers know they were changing the way absences were managed.

They also relied on teams at individual locations. In addition to its 22 manufacturing sites, Osram Sylvania maintains a customer-service center, a headquarters operation, three distribution centers and Sylvania Lighting Services, which has 30 branch offices nationwide with 5 to 20 on-the-road employees servicing retail and industry customers.

At each location, Chambers and Sheedy set up regional training sessions to educate the managers on the new programs. Then managers spelled out the program to workers and offered guidance on how to use it. The process was handled in stages because it was a lot to absorb, the two say.

Sheedy and Chambers aren't basking in their short-term success. Year one focused on "stopping the hemorrhage." Year two, they say, will focus on assessing absence and discipline policies, trying to simplify things and make the process uniform.

Tips

人力资源管理常用专业术语：

action learning：行动学习

alternation ranking method：交替排序法

annual bonus：年终分红

application forms：工作申请表

appraisal interview：评价面试

aptitudes：资质

arbitration：仲裁

attendance incentive plan：参与式激励计划

authority：职权

behavior modeling：行为模拟

behaviorally anchored rating scale (bars)：行为锚定等级评价法

benchmark job：基准职位

benefits：福利

bias：个人偏见

boycott：联合抵制

bumping/layoff procedures：工作替换/临时解雇程序

burnout：耗竭

candidate-order error：候选人次序错误

capital accumulation program：资本积累方案

career anchors：职业锚

career cycle：职业周期

career planning and development：职业规划与职业发展

case study method：案例研究方法

central tendency：居中趋势

citations：传讯

Civil Rights Act：民权法案

classes：类

classification (or grading) method：归类（或分级）法
collective bargaining：集体谈判
comparable worth：可比价值
compensable factor：报酬因素
computerized forecast：计算机化预测
content validity：内容效度
criterion validity：效标效度
critical incident method：关键事件法
Davis-Bacon Act (DBA)：戴维斯-佩根法案
day-to-day-collective bargaining：日常集体谈判
decline stage：下降阶段
deferred profit-sharing plan：延期利润分享计划
defined benefit：固定福利
defined contribution：固定缴款
Department of Labor job analysis：劳工部工作分析法
discipline：纪律
dismissal：解雇；开除
downsizing：精简
early retirement window：提前退休窗口
economic strike：经济罢工
Edgar Schein：艾德加·施恩
employee compensation：职员报酬
employee orientation：雇员上岗引导
Employee Retirement Income Security Act (ERISA)：雇员退休收入保障法案
employee services benefits：雇员服务福利
employee stock ownership plan (ESOP)：雇员持股计划
Equal Pay Act：公平工资法
establishment stage：确立阶段
exit interviews：离职面谈
expectancy chart：期望图表

experimentation：实验
exploration stage：探索阶段
eact-finder：调查
eair day's work：公平日工作
Fair Labor Standards Act：公平劳动标准法案
flexible benefits programs：弹性福利计划
flex place：弹性工作地点
flextime：弹性工作时间
forced distribution method：强制分布法
four-day workweek：每周4天工作制
Frederick Taylor：弗雷德里克·泰罗
functional control：职能控制
functional job analysis：功能性工作分析法
general economic conditions：一般经济状况
golden offerings：高龄给付
good faith bargaining：真诚的谈判
grade description：等级说明书
grades：等级
graphic rating scale：图尺度评价法
grid training：方格训练
grievance：抱怨
grievance procedure：抱怨程序
group life insurance：团体人寿保险
group pension plan：团体退休金计划
growth stage：成长阶段
guarantee corporation：担保公司
guaranteed fair treatment：有保证的公平对待
guaranteed piecework plan：有保障的计件工资制
gain sharing：收益分享
halo effect：晕轮效应

Health Maintenance Organization (HMO)：健康维持组织
illegal bargaining：非法谈判项目
impasse：僵持
implied authority：隐含职权
incentive plan：激励计划
individual retirement account (IRA)：个人退休账户
in-house development center：企业内部开发中心
insubordination：不服从
insurance benefits：保险福利
interviews：谈话；面谈
job analysis：工作分析
job description：工作描述
job evaluation：职位评价
job instruction training (JIT)：工作指导培训
job posting：工作公告
job rotation：工作轮换
job sharing：工作分组
job specifications：工作说明书
John Holland：约翰·霍兰德
junior board：初级董事会
layoff：临时解雇
leader attach training：领导者匹配训练
lifetime employment without guarantees：无保证终身解雇
line manager：直线管理者
local market conditions：地方劳动力市场
lockout：闭厂
maintenance stage：维持阶段
management assessment center：管理评价中心
management by objectives (MBO)：目标管理法
management game：管理竞赛
management grid：管理方格训练

Unit 8

Advertising and Publicity

Text A Internet Advertising

> 导读：广告是为了某种特定的需要，通过一定形式的媒体，公开而广泛地向公众传递信息的宣传手段。其中狭义的广告指经济广告，又称商业广告，是指以盈利为目的的广告，通常是商品生产者、经营者和消费者之间沟通信息的重要手段，或企业占领市场、推销产品、提供劳务的重要形式，主要目的是扩大经济效益。在21世纪这个信息化的时代，网络广告将成为未来广告的一种主流趋势。

  The future, noted William Gibson, a science-fiction writer, is already here—it is just unevenly distributed. To see the future of mobile phones, people look to Japan; to see the impact of broadband internet connections, they look to Republic of Korea. And for a glimpse of the future of advertising, the place to look appears to be Britain. The country is a "test bed" according to Eric Schmidt, chief executive of Google, which has just announced an alliance with British Sky Broadcasting (BSkyB), a British pay-television company. On December 6th the two companies announced that the Internet search and advertising giant would provide its search, E-mail, video and advertising services to BSkyB's broadband internet-service customers, with the aim of extending the partnership to BSkyB's main television business.

  Why Britain? The country has several factors in its favour. For a start, the British online-advertising market is "exploding", said Mr. Schmidt. The Internet accounts for 14% of companies' total spending on advertising in Britain, compared with about 5% worldwide (see chart). Expenditure on the Internet advertising in America is similar to that in Britain, but Britain's growth rates are slightly higher. In the first half of this year online advertising increased by 40% in Britain and 37% in America compared with the same period last year, according to the Internet Advertising Bureau, an industry body. Britain is now the leading market for online advertising, says Rob Noss, European chief executive of MindShare Interaction, a new-media subsidiary of WPP, a British advertising giant.

That is due, in part, to the presence of the BBC, Britain's state-controlled main broadcaster, which has no advertising. As a result, British companies spend less on television advertising than those in countries with big commercial broadcasters, and more on other types—which, in recent years, has meant online advertising. GroupM, the media-buying division of WPP, forecasts a 2.4% decline in British television advertising in 2006 and a flat market for 2007.

Eventually, says Sir Martin Sorrell, chief executive of WPP, the Internet will grow to account for 20% of worldwide advertising spending, at the expense of traditional media (broadcast and cable TV, print, radio and outdoor advertising). But Britain will reach this

point by 2009, predicts ZenithOptimedia, a market-research firm, at which point Internet advertising will be worth almost as much as television advertising. Britain has, in effect, got a head start over other countries as advertising spending shifts from old to new media.

Another catalyst of the growth of online advertising is Britons' enthusiasm for fast, always-on broadband connections to the Internet and for online shopping. In Britain 47% of households have broadband, compared with 44% in America and 33% in Germany. Consumers with broadband tend to shop online more frequently and spend more money than those with slower dial-up Internet connections. In the first six months of this year online retail-spending in Britain increased by 40% compared with the same period last year. The attraction of online ads is obvious.

Advertisers are waking up to the fact that British consumers typically spend a quarter of their media-consumption time on the Internet, says Linus Gregoriadis, an analyst at

Econsultancy.com, an Internet-research firm. Britons spend an average of 23 hours a week online, compared with 14 hours per week for Americans. Advertisers also like the efficiency of the medium: much of the advertising on the net is "pay-per-click", which means that advertisers pay only when consumers click on an ad, so they can be relatively confident that their advertisements are reaching a receptive audience. Mr. Noss says that several of his firm's clients already spend 40% of their advertising budgets online.

Blue-chip companies have yet to take the plunge and still spend only a tiny fraction of their budgets on Internet advertising, but that could be about to change. Unilever, an Anglo-Dutch consumer-goods giant, Heineken, Europe's largest brewer, and Procter & Gamble, a large consumer-goods company and the biggest advertiser worldwide, recently announced that they will switch a big chunk of their British advertising budgets away from television. Much of it will go online.

Britain is also attractive to advertisers because it is a homogeneous market, so there is no need to tailor advertisements for different parts of the country. The adoption of digital television is proceeding well, and BSkyB's platform is particularly advanced; Google and BSkyB plan to send advertisements to viewers' set-top boxes and then play them in commercial breaks depending on their interests, thus extending its targeted advertising model from the Internet into television.

And British consumers' relative enthusiasm for accessing the Internet from mobile phones—if not in the same league as that of Asian consumers—explains why Yahoo!, another big Internet firm, struck a deal last month with Vodafone, a big mobile operator based in Britain, to test new models for phone-based advertising. In addition, next year a new mobile-phone service for young people, called Blyk, will be launched in Britain before being rolled out across Europe. Users will be able to earn airtime in exchange for receiving advertisements on their handsets.

Blyk's co-founder, Pekka Ala-Pietila, a former president of Nokia, the world's biggest handset-maker, says the firm decided to launch in Britain first because it is the second-largest advertising market in the world after America, with sophisticated advertisers who appreciate the market segmentation that new technology makes possible. As a result, he says, Britain "is where we could learn the most". It all makes a welcome change for Britons used to hearing that their once-great country no longer leads the world in anything.

Notes:

1. British Sky Broadcasting（BSkyB）（英国天空广播有限公司）: British Sky Broadcasting Group (a. k. a. BSkyB; trading as Sky) is a public satellite broadcasting company operating in the United Kingdom and Ireland. It is the largest pay-TV broadcaster in the United Kingdom with over 10 million subscribers. British Sky Broadcasting was formed in 1990 by the equal merger of Sky Television and British Satellite Broadcasting.

2. WPP（英国WPP集团）: WPP plc (LSE: WPP, NASDAQ: WPPGY) is a global communications services company with its main management office in London, United Kingdom and its executive office in Dublin, Republic of Ireland. It is the world's largest advertising company measured by revenues, and has over 2,400 offices in 107 countries. It owns a number of advertising, public relations and market research networks, including Grey, Burson-Marsteller, Hill & Knowlton, JWT, Ogilvy Group, TNS and Young & Rubicam. Its primary listing is on the London Stock Exchange and it is a constituent of the FTSE 100 Index. It has a secondary listing on NASDAQ.

3. BBC（英国广播公司）: The British Broadcasting Corporation (BBC) is the principal state-owned public service broadcaster in the United Kingdom, headquartered in the Broadcasting House in the City of Westminster, London. It is the largest broadcaster in the world, with about 23,000 staff. Its main responsibility is to provide public service broadcasting in the United Kingdom, Channel Islands and Isle of Man. The BBC is an autonomous public service broadcaster that operates under a Royal Charter. Within the United Kingdom its work is funded principally by an annual television licence fee, which is charged to all United Kingdom households, companies and organisations using any type of equipment to record and/or receive live television broadcasts; the level of the fee is set annually by the British Government and agreed by Parliament.

Words & Expressions:

1. glimpse [glimps] n. 一瞥，一看
   vi. 瞥见
   vt. 瞥见
2. unevenly [ˈʌniːvənli] adv. 不均衡地；不平坦地；不平行地
3. distribute [diˈstribjuːt] vt. 分配；散布；分开；把……分类
4. expenditure [iksˈpenditʃə] n. 支出，花费；经费，消费额
5. subsidiary [səbˈsidiəri] adj. 附属的；辅助的
   n. 子公司；辅助者
6. division [diˈviʒən] n. 除法；部门；分割；师（军队）；[体]赛区
7. catalyst [ˈkætəlist] n. [物化]催化剂；刺激因素
8. broadband [ˈbrɔːdbænd] n. 宽频；宽波段
   adj. 宽频带的；宽波段的；宽频通信的
9. dial-up [ˈdaiəlʌp] n. [计][通信] 拨号（上网）
10. consumption [kənˈsʌmpʃən] n. 消费；消耗；肺痨
11. efficiency [iˈfiʃənsi] n. 效率；效能；功效
12. receptive [riˈseptiv] adj. 善于接受的；能容纳的
13. blue-chip [ˈbluːtʃip] adj. 第一流的；靠得住的；独特的；蓝色筹码的
14. plunge [plʌndʒ] n. 投入；跳进
    vi. 投入；陷入；跳进
    vt. 使陷入；使投入；使插入
15. brewer [ˈbruːə] n. 啤酒制造者；阴谋家
16. chunk [tʃʌŋk] n. 大块；矮胖的人或物
17. homogeneous [ˌhoməˈdʒiːniəs] adj. 均匀的；[数] 齐次的；同种的
18. set-top (box) n. 机顶（盒）
19. league [liːg] n. 联盟；社团；范畴
    vt. 使……结盟；与……联合
    vi. 团结；结盟

20. airtime [ˈɛəˌtaim] n. 电影或电视节目开始的时间
21. handset [ˈhændset] n. 手机，电话听筒
22. sophisticate [səˈfistikeit] vt. 弄复杂；使变得世故；曲解
    n. 久经世故的人；精通者
    vi. 诡辩
23. segmentation [ˌsegmənˈteiʃən] n. 分割；割断；细胞分裂

Exercises:

I. **Fill in the blanks with the suitable words given in the box. Change the form when necessary.**

| efficiency | league | receptive | distribute | unevenly |
| expenditure | plunge | subsidiary | sophisticate | consumption |

1. Payments have been _____ spread over commodities, countries, and time.
2. The books in the library were _____ according to subjects.
3. An announcement of further cuts in government _____ is imminent.
4. The business operation period of a _____ of a foreign insurance company shall start from the date of establishment of the _____.
5. I always take fuel _____ into consideration when buying a car.
6. They should be _____, appreciative, and fair when dealing with employee's suggestions.
7. Francis I's own _____ into Italy ended in his defeat and capture at the battle of Pavia.
8. The police suspected that the bank clerk was in _____ with the rubbers.
9. The relation of the literature and history were presented by way of entwine mutually of _____.
10. Such action can be justified on the grounds of greater _____.

II. Decide whether the following statements are true (T) or false (F) according to the passage.

1. In the future, the advertising will be distributed to every region in the world averagely. (   )
2. To see the future of mobile phones, people look to Republic of Korea; to see the impact of broadband internet connections, they look to Japan. (   )
3. British companies are spending more and more on online advertising in recent years, exceeding those countries with big commercial broadcasters. (   )
4. "Pay-per-click" means that advertisers pay only when consumers click on an ad, so they can be relatively confident that their advertisements are reaching a receptive audience. (   )
5. Britain is an uneven market; one should tailor advertisements for different parts of the country. (   )

Text B   Beijing Tries to Push Beyond "Made in China"

> 导读：中国是世界第一大出口国，世界第二大经济体。在中国国际影响力增强的同时，全球品牌的缺失威胁着中国成为商品进出口超级大国的梦想。如何在国际市场上扩大中国制造品牌的知名度，如何打造中国企业全球化，这不仅需要企业提高产品质量，加大本土产品的宣传力度，更需要企业能够放眼世界，不断提升其创新能力和合作精神。

Quick: Think of a Chinese brand name. Japan has Sony. Mexico has Corona. Germany has BMW. Republic of Korea has Samsung.

And China has ...?

If you're stumped, you're not alone. And for China, that is an enormous problem.

Last year, China overtook Germany to become the world's largest exporter, and this year it could surpass Japan as the world's No. 2 economy. But as China gains international heft, its lack of global brands threatens its dream of becoming a superpower.

No big marquee brands means China is stuck doing the global grunt work in factory cities while designers and engineers overseas reap the profits. Much of Apple's iPhone, for example, is made in China. But if a high-end version costs $750, China is lucky to hold on to $25. For a pair of Nikes, it's four pennies on the dollar.

"We've lost a bucket load of money to foreigners because they have brands and we don't," complained Fan Chunyong, the secretary general of the China Industrial Overseas Development and Planning Association. "Our clothes are Italian, French, German, so the profits are all leaving China ... We need to create brands, and fast."

The problem is exacerbated by China's lack of successful innovation and its reliance on stitching and welding together products that are imagined, invented and designed by others. A failure to innovate means China is trapped paying enormous amounts in patent royalties and licensing fees to foreigners who are.

China's government has responded in typically lavish fashion, launching a multibillion-dollar effort to create brands, encourage innovation and protect its market from foreign domination.

Through tax breaks and subsidies, China has embraced what it calls "a going-out strategy," backing firms seeking to buy foreign businesses, snap up natural resources or expand their footprint overseas.

Domestically, it has launched the "indigenous innovation" program to encourage its companies to manufacture high-tech goods by forcing foreign firms to hand over their trade secrets and patents if they want to sell their products there.

Since 2007, thousands of Chinese businessmen have attended government-sponsored seminars on "going out" learning everything from how to do battle with domineering Americans and Britons during conference calls to why a Chinese boss should think twice about publicly humiliating his wayward foreign workers—as he'd do to his staff at home.

China has also moved to rebrand China itself. Late last year, when memories of China's poisoned pet food and deadly milk were still fresh, the Ministry of Commerce contracted with the global advertising giant DDB for a $300,000 ad showing a series of high-tech products, from top-of-the-line running shoes to an iPod. As a guitar wails, a voice intones: "When it says "Made in China," what it really means is made in China, made with the world."

Remaining insular

In recent months, the Western media have hyperventilated with stories about China's going-out strategy and about Chinese firms buying up the globe—Oil! Gas! Cars!—and even investing in the United States. In 2000, China had $28 billion in overseas investments; this year, it could break $200 billion.

But a little perspective: Even if China's total foreign direct investment hits $200 billion, it still pales in comparison to smaller economies, such as Singapore's, Russia's and Brazil's. And China has plunked down only about $17 billion in rich countries, equivalent to the overseas assets of a single medium-ranked Fortune 500 company.

The 34 Chinese companies on the Fortune 500 list basically operate in China only. The world's three biggest banks are Chinese, but none is among the world's top 50, ranked by the extent of their geographical spread.

"Moving forward another 10 years," said Kenneth J. DeWoskin, chairman of Deloitte's China Research and Insight Center, "it's hard to see how viable Chinese companies will be if they just stay in China." China's attempts to fight what it sees as the stranglehold of foreign patents and intellectual property rights have also had hiccups.

China is estimated to have paid foreign firms more than $100 billion in royalties to use mobile telephone technology developed in the West, according to executives of Western communications companies.

So in the late 1990s, it decided to develop its own. But after more than $30 billion in development costs, its unique technology still has fewer than 20 million users in a market of more than 500 million.

Handset makers have told China's government that they won't produce phones equipped with the new technology unless they are given subsidies. And China has resorted to giving away the technology to Romania and Republic of Korea to encourage broader use.

"China is still stuck," said Joerg Wuttke, former president of the European Union Chamber of Commerce in China and a 25-year veteran of doing business in China. "There is a huge disconnect between the money spent in universities and the lack of products."

China also faces enormous challenges to creating globalized firms. Studies of Chinese executives show that they spend far more time with government officials—who in China are the key to their profits—than with customers, who are the key to international success.

"Chinese executives like me need to spend a generation outside China to learn how business is done around the world," said Hua Dongyi, who chairs a massive Chinese mining company in Australia but has also built roads in Algeria and infrastructure in Sudan. That's definitely true for Hua. In April, he was forced to apologize to his Australian workers after he told Chinese media that the workers were money-grubbing and lacked the "loyalty and sense of responsibility existing in many Chinese enterprises."

Lenovo's lessons

The Chinese computer maker-Lenovo, which bought IBM's ThinkPad in 2004, wasn't the first Chinese company to acquire a big foreign brand, but it's still considered the pioneer.

That's probably because China's other forays into buying foreign brands have ended in disaster. An attempt by the Chinese electronics firm TCL to become the world's biggest TV manufacturer in 2003 fizzled when its French subsidiary lost $250 million.

A move by a private Chinese company to take over a once-dominant U. S. lawn mower company, Murray Outdoor Power Equipment, ended in bankruptcy because, among other mistakes, the Chinese firm didn't realize that Americans tend to buy mowers mostly in the spring.

Lenovo purchased IBM's laptop division for $1.25 billion—a gutsy move considering that IBM's renowned ThinkPad brand lost $1 billion from 2000—2004, twice Lenovo's total profit during that time.

Although Lenovo's move was portrayed by many in the West as a sign of China's rise, Lenovo acted out of desperation, said Yang Yuanqing, who has been a senior executive at Lenovo since it was founded in the 1980s with government funds.

Lenovo was losing market share in China. Its technology was middling. It had no access to foreign markets. With one swoop, Lenovo internationalized, purchased a famous brand and got a warehouse of technology as well.

But from the start, things were tough.

Lenovo's American competitors fanned anti-Chinese flames in Congress, insinuating that Lenovo could insert spyware into the computers it was selling to the U. S. government. The firm also faced enormous challenges bridging cultural divides among U. S. workers at its Raleigh, N. C., headquarters, the Japanese who made ThinkPads and the Chinese who made Lenovos.

William Amelio, the firm's second chief executive who had been lured from a top job at Dell, remembers his first trip to Beijing as the new Lenovo boss in late 2005.

"I was greeted with rose petals and the red carpet treatment and company songs. In Raleigh, everyone's arms were crossed. It was like, 'Who died and left you the boss?'" he said. "You had the respect for power in the East and the disdain for authority in the West."

Lenovo responded by following the lead of an increasing number of Chinese firms: returning to its roots. Yang Yuanqing was reappointed its chief executive and refocused Lenovo on the company's one bright spot: the China market. Sales skyrocketed, despite lackluster performance overseas.

Lenovo, according to Bob O' Donnell, a longtime expert on personal computers at IDC, "became a Chinese company again."

Still, analysts said Lenovo's rocky foreign adventure saved the company.

Lenovo might not have much of a brand overseas, but its association with a foreign firm has helped it in China. Lenovo's computers routinely command twice the price in China that they do in the United States. Lenovo offers its top-of-the-line ThinkPad W700 to the Chinese government at $12,500; in the United States, it runs for $2,500.

Chinese officials pushing the "going-out" strategy have looked at Lenovo as a model for

Chinese firms seeking to become known multinational brands. But for China's companies, going out might be the secret to staying alive at home.

This year, the Chinese car company Geely bought Volvo from Ford. Pundits figured it was to expand China's economic heft—and its brands—overseas. But as Geely's founder, Li Shufu, put it, "Volvo will find a new home market in China."

Notes:

Yang Yuanqing（杨元庆）: born 1964, is the current chief executive officer of Lenovo. He was a board chairman of Lenovo from 2004—2008. Before the acquisition of IBM PC division by Lenovo in 2004, he was the President and CEO of the company. One of his major achievements has been making Lenovo the best-selling PC brand in China since 1997. In 2001, Business Week named him as one of the rising stars in Asia.

Words & Expressions:

1. marquee [mɑːˈkiː] n. 选取框；大天幕；华盖
2. grunt [grɔnt] n. 工作乏味收入低的工人
3. exacerbate [ekˈsæsəbeit] vt. 使加剧；使恶化；激怒
4. snap up 抢购，匆匆吃下，抢先弄到手；锁键调节式
5. indigenous [inˈdidʒinəs] adj. 本土的；土著的；国产的；固有的
6. hyperventilate [haipəˈventileit] vi. 强力呼吸；换气过度

　　　　　　　　　　　　　　　　vt. 使强力呼吸（喻）言过其实，夸夸其谈地说
7. plunk down 重金买下，付钱买
8. stranglehold [ˈstræŋglhəuld] n. 束缚；压制
9. hiccup [ˈhikʌp] n. 小问题，暂时性耽搁
10. royalty [ˈrɔiəlti] n. 皇室；版税；王权；专利税

11. foray ['fɔrei] n. 突袭；侵略；攻击
                  vi. 袭击
                  vt. 劫掠；（改变职业、活动的）尝试
12. middling ['midliŋ] n. 中级品
                  adj. 中等的；第二流的
                  adv. 中等
                  v. 把……放在中间
13. swoop [swu:p] vi. 猛扑；突然袭击；突然下降；飞扑
                  n. 猛扑；俯冲；突然袭击
                  vt. 攫取；抓去
14. insinuate [in'sinjueit] vt. 暗示；使逐渐而巧妙地取得；使迂回地潜入
                  vi. 暗讽；说含沙射影的话
15. lackluster ['læk,lʌstə] n. 无光泽；暗淡
                  adj. 无光泽的；平凡的

Exercises:

I. **Fill in the blanks with the suitable words or expressions given in the box. Change the form when necessary.**

| insinuate | middling | stranglehold | lackluster |
| indigenous | royalty | snap up | exacerbate |

1. WaterAid is an international charity dedicated to helping people escape the _____ of poverty and disease caused by living without safe water and sanitation.
2. Computer viruses are sneaky programs designed to _____ their way into your computer, copy themselves, spread to other computers and, usually, cause a few symptoms.
3. They have jobs of _____ status, perhaps in retail or self-employed manual trades.

4. _____ progress reports not hearing feedback from a supervisor is a good way to tell if your work has become routine.

5. Some performance appraisal systems may then _____ the situation, for instance, by forcing employees or groups to be ranked.

6. In the long term, we also seek opportunities to work hand in hand with Christian formal education centers to provide quality training for _____ organizations/churches.

7. The term "return" means the amount yielded by investments, such as profits, dividends, interests, _____ or other legitimate income.

8. All around the country, bargain hunters are rushing to _____ discounted versions of the season's most popular items and industry analysts expect robust sales overall.

II. Read the following text and choose the best sentence from A to E below to fill in each of the gaps in the text.

China is the world's largest shoemaker and exporter. But it must step out of its reputation as a cheap shoemaker. To achieve that goal, Chinese shoemakers should enhance their shoemaking technologies, improve their brands and begin exporting to more regions.

More than two-thirds of the 6 billion pairs of shoes produced last year in China were exported. Export volumes of Chinese-made shoes exceeded U.S. $10 billion. (1) _____ Leather shoes sold for U. S. $5.50 per pair.

Low-grade shoes account for most of China's exports of shoes. Prices of Chinese-made shoes are lower than those manufactured in Brazil, South Korea and Thailand. Chinese-made shoes tend to cost less than shoes manufactured by rising exporters such as Viet Nam. (2) _____ Chinese shoemakers produce a combined 12 billion pairs of shoes per year, and oversupplies have left China's shoemakers heavily reliant on shoe dealers who often choose account sales to reduce risks.

But most domestic producers have failed to improve quality and upgrade their designs to increase competitiveness. Rather, they have begun focusing on the export market, where payments for their goods are generally ensured. (3) _____ As a result, Chinese shoes are running towards international markets. China has few large shoe manufacturers. Most export

U. S. $100,000 worth of shoes per year. These small shoe exporters commonly adopt low-price strategies, which result in decreased export prices of their shoes. Overproduction and the debut of numerous small shoe exporters exacerbated the situation.

In addition, China's shoemakers have long neglected research, development and design. (4) _____ Chinese shoemakers also lack necessary information about international markets. Their technologies also lag behind those of their international counterparts. As a result, Chinese shoemakers and exporters have lingered in the low-end shoe market. Unable to open new markets, they become used to concentrating on markets filled by other Chinese shoemakers. (5) _____ Meanwhile, other markets, such as South America, Russia and Africa, have been neglected by China's shoe manufacturers.

A. Also, shoemakers receive tax breaks on their exports.
B. However, the average price of each pair of shoes China exported was U. S. $2.40.
C. Overproduction is the main reason for the lower prices of Chinese shoes in the international market.
D. Such overseas markets as Japan and the United States, have become saturated with Chinese shoes.
E. They have for years received orders to produce existing styles or to copy others' designs.

III. Translate the following sentences into Chinese.

1. The problem is exacerbated by China's lack of successful innovation and its reliance on stitching and welding together products that are imagined, invented and designed by others.
2. A failure to innovate means China is trapped paying enormous amounts in patent royalties and licensing fees to foreigners who are.
3. In recent months, the Western media have hyperventilated with stories about China's "going-out strategy" and about Chinese firms buying up the globe—Oil! Gas! Cars!—and even investing in the United States.
4. China's attempts to fight what it sees as the stranglehold of foreign patents and intellectual property rights have also had hiccups.

5. Chinese officials pushing the "going-out" strategy have looked at Lenovo as a model for Chinese firms seeking to become known multinational brands. But for China's companies, going out might be the secret to staying alive at home.

Supplementary Reading

The Harder Hard Sell

More people are rejecting traditional sales messages, presenting the ad industry with big challenges.

It may have been Lord Leverhulme, the British soap pioneer, Frank Woolworth, America's first discount-retailer, or John Wanamaker, the father of the department store; are all said to have complained that they knew half of their advertising budget was wasted, but didn't know which half. As advertising starts to climb out of its recent slump, the answer to their problem is easier to find as the real effects of advertising become more measurable. But that is exposing another, potentially more horrible truth, for the $1 trillion advertising and marketing industry: in some cases, it can be a lot more than half of the client's budget that is going down the drain.

The advertising industry is passing through one of the most disorienting periods in its history. This is due to a combination of long-term changes, such as the growing diversity of media, and the arrival of new technologies, notably the Internet. Consumers have become better informed than ever before, with the result that some of the traditional methods of advertising and marketing simply no longer work.

Ad spending grew rapidly in the late 1990s, but in 2000—

just as the technology bubble was about to burst—it soared by more than 8% in America, which represents about half the world market. The following year it plunged by 8%. Spending is up again, according to ZenithOptimedia, which has long tracked the industry. It forecasts that worldwide expenditure in 2004 on major media (newspapers, magazines, television, radio, cinema, outdoor and the Internet) will grow by 4.7% to $343 billion. It will be helped by a collection of big events, including the European football championship, the Olympic Games and an election in America. Historically, when there is an upturn in advertising expenditure, it tends to rise faster than the wider economy. So, provided economic growth can be sustained, ad spending may continue to pick up.

How will the money be spent? There are plenty of alternatives to straightforward advertising, including a myriad of marketing and communications services, some of which are called "below-the-line" advertising. They range from public relations to direct mail, consumer promotions (such as coupons), in-store displays, business-to-business promotions (like paying a retailer for shelf-space), telemarketing, exhibitions, sponsoring events, product placements and more.

These have become such an inseparable part of the industry that big agencies now provide most of them. Although some are less than glamorous, marketing services have grown more quickly than advertising. Ads in the cost of market research, and this part of the industry was worth some $750 billion worldwide last year, estimates WPP, one of the world's biggest advertising and marketing groups.

As ever, the debate in the industry centres on the best way to achieve results. Is it more cost-effective, for instance, to employ a PR agency to invite a journalist out to lunch and persuade him to write about a product than to pay for a display ad in that journalist's newspaper? Should you launch a new car with glossy magazine ads, or—as some carmakers now do—simply park demonstration models in shopping malls and motorway service stations? And is it better to buy a series of ads on a specialist cable-TV channel or splurge $2.2 million on a single 30-second commercial during this year's Super Bowl?

Such decisions are ever harder to make. Although a Super Bowl ad is still cheaper than in 2000, in general network-TV pricing has risen faster than inflation—even though fewer people tune in. Changes in TV-viewing habits, however, are only part of a much wider shift in the way media is consumed, not least because it has become more fragmented and diverse.

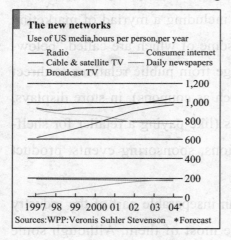

For a start, people are spending less time reading newspapers and magazines, but are going to the cinema more, listening to more radio and turning in ever-increasing numbers to a new medium, the Internet.

After the technology bust, it was easy to dismiss the Internet. But the phenomenal success of many e-commerce firms, such as Amazon and eBay, shows that millions of people are becoming comfortable buying goods and services online. Many more are using the Internet to research products, services and prices for purchases made offline. Some 70% of new-car buyers in America, for instance, use websites to determine which vehicle to buy—and often to obtain competing quotes from dealers.

Google that

Such consumers can be targeted by internet advertisers and, in some cases, their responses accurately measured. A surge in online advertising is being led by paid-for text-links dished up by search engines such as Google and Yahoo! The response rate from people clicking on paid links can be as low as 1%—about the same as direct mail, which remains one of the biggest forms of advertising. But there is an important difference: Internet advertisers usually pay only if someone clicks on their link. This is the equivalent of paying for the delivery of junk mail only to households that read it.

How are companies and the advertising industry responding to these trends in media consumption? Some people do not believe they amount to a sea-change, while others are simply hoping it will not come to pass on their watch, reckons Sir Martin Sorrell, WPP's chief executive.

Nor is it the only significant force he sees at work. New markets, such as China, are becoming increasingly important for advertisers, especially multinationals. But these markets can have very different characteristics. Clients are also more concerned than ever about getting value for money. What will increasingly matter, says Sir Martin, is not what it costs to put an ad in front of 1,000 people (a traditional industry measure), but "how effective is that cost-per-thousand?"

At the same time, negotiating advertising deals is becoming tougher because of consolidation, both among clients and among media owners. This could favour the big, integrated agencies. In May, WPP won a contract to handle all the advertising and marketing for HSBC, after the international banking group decided that parent companies and not their individual agencies should bid for the $600 million it spends on such services every year. Samsung, a big South Korean electronics firm, is also expected to appoint a single group.

Nevertheless, the smaller agencies believe they can still compete by being more nimble. "There is definitely a change in the landscape," says Jane Asscher, chairman of 23rd, a London-based agency that describes itself as "media-neutral" in its choice of outlets for campaigns. Ms. Asscher believes that consumers are becoming far more sophisticated in their reaction to all forms of advertising and marketing, so smarter ways have to be used to reach them.

During the slump, some companies tried different forms of advertising and liked the response they got. "There's lots of ways to skin a cat today," says Scott Goodson, founder of StrawberryFrog, an agency based in Amsterdam that specialises in international campaigns. While his firm still uses traditional media, such as TV and print, it is often in conjunction with other techniques, such as "viral" marketing. This means trying to spread the message by word of mouth—still considered the most-powerful form of advertising. Sometimes that involves using the Internet for E-mail messages containing jokes, film clips and games, which recipients are encouraged to pass along to friends.

No one knows just how important the Internet will eventually be as an advertising medium. Some advertisers think it will be a highly cost-effective way of reaching certain groups of consumers—especially for small companies operating in niche businesses. But not everyone uses the Internet, and nor is it seen as particularly good at brand building. Barry Diller, the head of InterActiveCorp, believes network TV is a great place to promote his company's websites, such as Expedia, his online travel agency, and LendingTree, a consumer lender. Unlike bricks-and-mortar businesses, web-based firms do not worry if their ad is being seen by lots of people in towns where they have no shops. They just want people to remember their website address—or at least enough of their name to be Googled.

So far, the Internet accounts for only a tiny slice of the overall advertising pie, although it has been growing rapidly. A joint study by the Interactive Adverti-sing Bureau and Price-waterhouse Coopers found that internet advertising revenue in America grew by 39% to $ 2.3 billion in the first quarter of 2004, compared with the same period a year earlier.

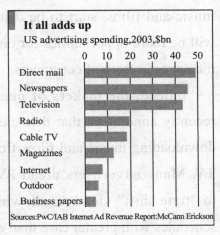

And Google and Yahoo! have yet to unleash the full potential of their technology. Google, which already places text ads on other people's websites and splits the revenue with them, recently, began testing a system to distribute display ads as well, in effect increasing its role as a sort of online ad agency.

Others are honing new techniques. As part of a recent campaign for American Airlines, the online edition of the *Wall Street Journal* used "behavioural targeting" to estimate how likely readers were to be frequent-flyers based on how much interest they paid to travel-related stories and columns. The targeted readers were presented with American Airline ads, and not just when they were reading travel stories. According to Revenue Science, a New York company that developed the targeting system, the results were dramatic: the number of business travelers who saw the ads more than doubled.

The potential for advertising on the Internet is tempting more firms to join the fray. For instance, Microsoft is working on a search system with the intention of leapfrogging Google. Microsoft and others see that as more types of media, including music and films, start to be distributed over the Internet, there will be more opportunities for online operators to put advertising messages in front of consumers.

Indeed, the makers of personal video recorders (PVRs) recently announced that their new machines will be capable of downloading music and films from the Internet, as well as from TV. Many advertisers dread PVRs because they can be used to "time shift" viewing, allowing viewers to record their own schedules with greater ease than existing video recorders. Several studies have shown that users think one of the machine's most—appealing features is the ability to skip past ads. The providers of internet-based content might be able to slip in those ads in other ways than traditional 30-second commercials, perhaps through sponsorship deals or as display ads on the websites which PVR owners will use to select their programming.

Bombarded

People are tiring of ads in all their forms. A recent study by Yankelovich Partners, an American marketing-services consultancy, says that consumer resistance to the growing intrusiveness of marketing and advertising has been pushed to an all-time high. Its study found 65% of people now feel "constantly bombarded" by ad messages and that 59% feel that ads have very little relevance to them. Almost 70% said they would be interested in products or services that would help them avoid marketing pitches.

It has been calculated that the average American is subjected to some 3,000 advertising messages every day. If you add in everything from the badges on cars to slogans on sweatshirts, the ads in newspapers, on taxis, in subways and even playing on TVs in lifts, then some people could be exposed to more than that number just getting to the office. No wonder many consumers seem to be developing the knack of tuning-out adverts.

"Consumers are getting harder to influence as commercial clutter invades their lives," says a recent report by Deutsche Bank. It examined the effectiveness of TV advertising on 23 new and mature brands of packaged goods and concluded that in some cases it was a waste of time. Although in the short-term TV advertising would lead to an incremental increase in volume sales in almost every case, there was only a positive cash return on that investment in 18% of cases. Over a longer term the picture improved, with 45% of cases showing a return on investment. Not surprisingly, new products did better than older ones. The study concluded that "increased levels of marketing spending were less important than having new items on the shelf and increasing distribution."

The effectiveness of advertising is a hugely controversial area. Conventional wisdom in the industry is that sales may well increase for a certain period even after the advertising of a product ends. But there comes a point when sales start to decline and it then becomes extremely expensive to rebuild the brand.

This supports the idea of continuous advertising. But some

people in the industry believe the conventional wisdom is no longer true. When America's big TV networks reached prime-time audiences of 90% of households, they were a powerful way to build a brand. Now that those audiences might be as low as one-third of households, other ways of promoting a brand have become more competitive. Moreover, many clients never really embraced continuous advertising: when times get tough, just as they did after 2000, one of the first things many companies cut is their ad budget.

Robert Shaw, a visiting professor at the Cranfield School of Management in Britain, runs a forum in which a number of big companies try to monitor the "marketing payback" from advertising. The return from traditional media was, he says, "never terribly good". Generally under half of ads provide a return on their investment. And there can be various reasons why ads influence sales, other than their direct effect on consumers. For instance, if a producer announces a multi-million dollar ad-campaign, then retailers are often persuaded to increase deliveries. This can result in a "distribution effect" that leads to additional sales.

Some companies have profited from reallocating their spending across different media, adds Mr. Shaw. But it is a tricky business to determine what works best. For many companies, and especially the media-buyers who purchase space and slots for ads, greater media diversity and the arrival of the Internet has made a difficult job much tougher.

Soap stars

Some big spenders have already made clear choices. With an annual budget of more than $4 billion, America's Procter & Gamble (P&G) is the biggest advertiser in the world. Ten years ago about 90% of its global ads spend were on TV. Now the figure is much smaller. Last year the company launched a non-prescription version of Prilosec, an anti-heartburn medicine. It was one of the most successful brand launches in the company's history, according to Jim Stengel, P&G's global marketing officer. But only about one-quarter of the marketing spend on Prilosec went to TV. The rest was spent on other forms of marketing, such as in-store promotions.

P&G, which helped to launch TV soap operas as a new way to market goods, is now looking once again for novel ways to reach consumers. Three years ago it set up an operation called Tremor to recruit an army of several hundred thousand American teenagers. It uses them to discuss ideas about new products and to help spread marketing messages. In return, the teenagers get to hear about and use new things before many of their peers.

Getting trendsetters to buy (or be given) new products in order to influence a broader market is hardly a new idea. So-called "early adopters" are a similar group, much sought-after by consumer-electronics companies in order to give their new products a good start. But there is a wider group which marketers sometimes call "prosumers"; short for proactive consumers. Some people in the industry believe this group is the most powerful of all.

Euro RSCG, a big international agency, is completing a nine-country study of prosumers, which it says can represent 20% or so of any particular group. They can be found everywhere, are at the vanguard of consumerism, and what they say to their friends and colleagues about brands and products tends to become mainstream six to eighteen months later. They also vary by category, says Marc Lepere, Euro RSCG's chief marketing officer: a wine prosumer, for instance, will not necessarily be a prosumer of cars.

Such people often reject traditional ads and invariably use the Internet to research what they are going to buy and how much they are going to pay for it. Half of prosumers distrust companies and products they cannot find on the Internet. If they want to influence prosumers, says Mr. Lepere, companies have to be extremely open about providing information.

Despite all of these complications, many in the advertising business remain sanguine. For Rupert Howell, chairman of the London arm of McCann Erickson, which is part of the giant Interpublic group, the industry's latest downturn was the third he has experienced. As it did from the others, he says, the industry is emerging a little wiser. But, he insists, "the underlying principles haven't changed." Even the arrival of new media, like the Internet, does not spell the demise of the old. Indeed, as he points out, TV never killed radio, which in turn never killed newspapers. They did pose huge creative challenges, but that's OK, he maintains: "The advertising industry is relentlessly inventive; that's what we do."

Tips

广告专业术语：

account executive (AE)：客户代表，或客户执行。代表广告公司接受广告主的各种业务，并负责整体执行的人。

account group：业务小组。广告公司内负责某特定客户的工作小组。以 AE 为中心，成员包括行销企划、创意、媒体等工作人员，替客户执行广告企划设定、广告表现制作、媒体安排等业务。

appeal point：诉求点。广告信息中，最能打动消费者心理，并引起行动的重点。

brain storming：头脑风暴。可自由想象，不受限制的讨论会议。

brand image：品牌形象。消费者对商品品牌之印象。

commercial film (CF)：广告影片，不是电视广告脚本。

commercial script：电视广告脚本。

competitive presentation：比稿。有的广告主不会将广告计划立即委托一家广告公司，而是让多家广告公司彼此竞争，从中选择最优秀、最满意的广告公司。

copywriter：文案（撰文人员）。负责广告文案的专门写作。

corporate identity (CI)：企业识别。以统一性的标志表示企业的理念、文化及经营的任务。

creative boutique：创意工作室。"boutique" 为法语中商店的意思，指专门零售店，特别是指贩卖流行物品、装饰品的商店。以这种语意为背景，由少数人组成、专门制作广告的公司，便称为小型制作专业广告公司。

direct response advertising：直效广告。需要从潜在客户处得到简单回应的广告。例如邮购、直接信函、电讯行销，以及有线电视购物频道。直效广告必须是双向沟通的。

director：指导。在整个广告作业中，担任指导的专业职务。依照其经验不同，指导可分为资深指导(senior director)、指导(director)和助理指导(assistant director)。

指导有以下各专业职位：

account director：业务指导

creative director：创意指导

arts director：美术指导

copy director：文案指导

media director：媒体指导

planning director：企划指导

finisher：完稿员。从事完成广告平面工作的人员。

layout：构图。版面设计之技巧。对美术设计而言，版面编排是一种基本技术。

presentation：提案。对客户做正式的广告战略及提出创意企划案。

public service advertising：公益广告。企业及各社会团体诉求公共服务内容的广告。公益广告的范围相当广泛，举凡社会、福祉、教育，甚至谋求国际相互了解的活动都囊括在内。

supervisor：总监。广告专业中的最高职位，其工作为带领整个专业团队。有以下各种专业总监：

    account supervisor：业务总监

    creative supervisor：创意总监

    media supervisor：媒体总监

    planning supervisor：企划总监

    research supervisor：调查总监

target market：目标市场。最主要的消费群。

traffic control specialist（一般简称 traffic）：制管人员。广告制作的流程及时间上的控制是非常重要的一件事，制管人员即负责推进及监督广告作业中各部门是否按照计划进行的专员。

Unit 9

Training

Text A Training the Trainer

> 导读：培训者，又可称作培训经理或培训专家，是指在培训与发展过程中具体承担培训任务，向受训者传授知识与技能的人。培训者通过建立企业培训体系，管理企业内外部培训资源，开发和独立授课，从人力资源培训团队的角度来支持一个团队的知识、技能结构，进而对于绩效起到辅助作用。培训者这一职务是西方管理学通过大量的实践和演化从人事管理范畴当中构建出来的。培训者的素质、能力深刻影响着培训活动的进程和效果，因此对培训者自身的训练与培养也至关重要。

When you're sitting in the audience listening to a subject matter expert, it's easy for your mind to suddenly wander to your grocery list, your child's play, or that new iPod—anything but the topic before you.

Even when a training session covers an important topic, is well organized, and is led by an expert, its delivery can be as dry as toast.

Not everyone who is asked to deliver training is a trainer, and yet, many are called on to act in that capacity. We all know someone who attended a class and was told to "come back and teach it to us," as though magically that person would become skilled and comfortable in their newfound role of trainer.

Frequently, the individual responsible for leading a training session is unaware of adult learning theory, or ways to increase Interest, enhance retention, and emphasize the applicability of course material. The newly appointed trainer may have never designed a curriculum or may tend to struggle with visual aids, yet we entrust them to the learner to facilitate, instruct, and teach.

A train-the-trainer class is beneficial whether one has presented on several occasions or lacks the skills and knowledge needed for an effective presentation. The instructional systems design model is based on the U. S. Navy's integrated approach to training (upon which I have expanded to include class-room management). It demonstrates in six modules what a train-the-trainer course should integrate into the learning experience. Each area within the instructional systems design model contributes to the learners' ability to receive, retain, and apply information.

The needs analysis assesses the aptitude of the learner and determines specific information required for him to perform his job. The needs analysis identifies what the learner already knows and the skills that are needed to enhance work performance. It is important for a trainer to be able to answer these questions because they will assist him in identifying where knowledge gaps are and how they can be addressed.

An analysis can be assessed in a variety of ways, including direct observation, questionnaires, consultation with persons in key positions, interviews, focus groups, surveys, tests, and work samples. Once it is determined that a need exists, the trainer must determine what the learning objectives will be. Learning objectives describe the intended result of the instruction, the conditions under which performance should take place, and how well the learner must perform.

To enhance effectiveness, the trainer should also assess the level of experience that the learner has in his field, his tenure with the organization, and any related skills or knowledge he possess.

Instructional design defines how a program is constructed to meet the needs of the learner. The learning professional has to be able to design an effective approach for the learner and respect that each learner's needs are different.

Design determines the content of the lesson and what the learner needs to know or do. An effective design includes a specific plan, with timeframes that allow the trainer to meet the needs of the organization and the individual learner.

The design should have an opening, which could include an icebreaker, introductions, an agenda, and a list of objectives. This should be followed by an explanation to the participant of what he is going to learn—this involves giving the big picture first, then moving from general ideas to more specific ones. Adult learning theory suggests that adults learn best from the most fundamental concepts to the most complex. The learning professional should never give everything at once, as it can be overwhelming for the learner.

Instruction delivery reflects the presentation skills of the learning professional and how the information is delivered. When the learning professional is designing the presentation, he should be mindful of how the learner will retain the information. For one, the generation of the learner is an important consideration for the trainer. Do they like the bells and whistles of slide presentations or do they find them to be distracting or a turn-off to learning?

In delivering the presentation, the trainer should always prepare the learner for what he will be learning. Studies have shown that it takes three times for information to actually stick. Tell the learner what he is going to learn; explain why the task is important; explain when and where the task is performed; and always define any terms, abbreviations, and acronyms that will be used, even if the learner is already perhaps familiar with them.

Information is more meaningful when—

A. A demonstration is provided.

B. Critical areas are identified.

C. Specific features are pointed out.

D. Examples are given.

E. Non-applicable examples and common errors or trouble spots are identified.

Have the learner practice in small steps first, and then perform the entire task. Correct errors if necessary, get the learner involved, and follow up with immediate feedback. Encourage questions and check for understanding by asking questions such as, "Why would this be important to know?" and "What do you think this means?" Offer examples in the form of real experiences to clarify a point, and identify and label important information.

There are a variety of instructional methods used to deliver information, and each has its own purpose.

The learning professional should determine when to use role play, lecturettes, lectures, case studies, and demonstrations. The instructional methodology must be appropriate for the information being presented, and at the same time, meet the learning style of the learner.

The trainer wants to ensure that the methodology used will be successful in transferring knowledge effectively. Demonstration and direct instruction are designed to assist the learner in retaining concepts and skills. Case studies are used to develop analytic and problem-solving skills. Mini lectures and discussions work best when time is limited, and both increase the learner's interpersonal skills.

Small-group discussion allows for greater participation, and learners often feel more comfortable. Ultimately, with each method, real situations should be practiced as much as possible. Deciding which method to use will depend on the learners and how they apply the information provided. One effective method of instruction is role play; however, very few people are comfortable with role play.

To help reduce anxiety about role playing, trainers can schedule the role play for later in the day or later on in the program; ask for volunteers ahead of time; provide a full explanation of the purpose and outcomes of the role play; and if appropriate, let participants develop their own situations.

Effective classroom management allows trainers to present material in a professional manner. Activities that occur in the classroom include creating introducing and closing material, setting the tone in the classroom, affirming the importance of energy boosters and breaks, anticipating and generating questions, pacing the material, and managing the various personalities of the participants.

Trainers should set the tone at the beginning of the class while the material is being introduced and the logistics shared. Participants can then be asked to place cell phones on vibrate, and to avoid sidebar conversations. Remind them that no questions are silly and to respect all learners.

The trainer can gauge the learner's perception of the program throughout the presentation. The learner's body language may be opened or closed; clues such as folded arms or lack of attention are additional signs. If participants are asking questions or relating experiences, this is an indication of interest and engagement.

Anticipate some of the questions that learners may have, involve the learner when questions are asked, and return the questions back to the class. By doing so, trainers are testing their knowledge while simultaneously responding to the questions.

Another key for trainers is to be honest. If the answer to a question is not known, encourage trainers to let the learner know that they will get back to him. Faster learners can assist slower learners.

Managing the classroom can be a daunting task, especially if the learners do not want to be there. Trainers should remember to never argue with participants and to keep the lesson moving toward its objectives. There might be someone who is constantly talking. The best way for a trainer to address this behavior is to ask that individual direct questions and stand near her (him).

Other common personalities include the naysayer—one who readily dismisses opinions of others. The best way for trainers to address this behavior is to cite facts or typical experiences of others. An appropriate response might begin, "I appreciate your experience. Studies show that ..."

Regarding individuals who engage in sidebar conversations, trainers can include them in the conversation, asking questions along the lines of, "Is there something you'd like to share with the class?"

Trainers should be sure to think about what they would do if the equipment were to malfunction, if the materials for the class did not arrive on time, or if some of the required materials weren't available.

Evaluation is an effective way of providing objective feedback to the learning professional. It is a way to determine whether you have accomplished what you set out to do and if the learner received the knowledge and skills he needed. In addition, this tool is a guide to assist learning professionals with future planning and next steps.

The trainer has a significant effect on the organization's cost savings. Therefore, when the novice trainer has received training herself, she is more comfortable, better prepared, and more knowledgeable about herself and the material.

Ultimately, a learning organization should ensure that each person given the marching orders to "come back and teach" will be well equipped to do so.

Notes:

iPod（苹果播放器）: iPod is a line of portable media players designed and marketed by Apple and launched on October 23, 2001. The product line-up currently consists of the hard drive-based iPod Classic, the touchscreen iPod Touch, the compact iPod Nano, and the ultra-compact iPod Shuffle. IPod Classic models store media on an internal hard drive, while all other models use flash memory to enable their smaller size (the discontinued Mini used a microdrive miniature hard drive). As with many other digital music players, iPods can also serve as external data storage devices. Storage capacity varies by model, ranging from 2 GB for the iPod Shuffle to 160 GB for the iPod Classic. All of the models have been redesigned multiple times since their introduction. The most recent iPod redesigns were introduced on September 1, 2010. Apple's iTunes software can be used to transfer music to the devices from computers using certain versions of Apple Macintosh and Microsoft Windows operating systems. For users who choose not to use iTunes or whose computers cannot run iTunes, several open source alternatives are available for the iPod. iTunes and its alternatives may also transfer photos, videos, games, contact information, E-mail settings, Web bookmarks, and calendars to iPod models supporting those features.

Words & Expressions：

1. retention [ri'tenʃən] n. 保留；扣留，滞留；记忆力
2. curriculum [kə'rikjuləm] n. 课程（复数为 curricula 或 lums）
3. facilitate [fə'siliteit] vt. 促进；帮助；使容易
4. demonstrate ['demənstreit] vt. 证明；展示；论证
   vi. 示威
5. module ['mɔdju:l] n. 模块；组件；模数
6. retain [ri'tein] vt. 保持；雇；记住
7. aptitude ['æptitju:d] n. 天资；自然倾向；适宜
8. tenure ['tenjuə] n. 任期；占有
   vt. 授予……终身职位
9. define [di'fain] vt. 定义；使明确；规定
10. overwhelming [,əuvə'hwelmiŋ] adj. 压倒性的；势不可当的
    v. 压倒；淹没（overwhelm 的 ing 形式）；制伏
11. abbreviation [ə,bri:vi'eiʃən] n. 缩写；缩写词
12. acronym ['ækrəunim] n. 首字母缩略词
13. clarify ['klærifai] vt. 澄清；阐明
    vi. 得到澄清；变得明晰；得到净化
14. affirm [ə'fə:m] vt. 肯定；断言
    vi. 确认；断言
15. methodology [,meθə'dɔlədʒi] n. 方法学，方法论
16. vibrate [vai'breit] vi. 振动；颤动；摇摆；踌躇
    vt. 使振动；使颤动
17. sidebar ['saidbɑ:] n. 工具条；侧边拦；其他选项
18. gauge [geidʒ] n. 计量器；标准尺寸；容量规格
    vt. 测量；估计；给……定规格
19. anticipate [æn'tisipeit] vt. 预期，期望；占先，抢先；提前使用
20. daunting ['dɔ:ntiŋ] adj. 使人畏缩的；使人气馁的；令人却步的
21. naysayer ['neiseiə] n. 否定者；拒绝者；老是唱反调的人

22. dismiss [dɪsˈmɪs] vt. 解散；解雇；开除；让……离开
    vi. 解散
23. novice [ˈnɒvɪs] n. 初学者，新手

Exercises:

Ⅰ. Match the words on the left with their meanings on the right.

1. aptitude   A. to make easy or easier; assist the progress of
2. tenure   B. to show clearly and deliberately; manifest
3. define   C. all the courses of study offered by an educational institution
4. anticipate   D. to keep or hold in a particular place, condition, or position
5. facilitate   E. an inherent ability, as for learning; a talent
6. curriculum   F. to describe the nature or basic qualities of; explain
7. retention   G. the act, fact, or condition of holding something in one's possession, as real estate or an office
8. demonstrate   H. to make clear or easier to understand; elucidate
9. clarify   I. an ability to recall or recognize what has been learned or experienced; memory
10. retain   J. to feel or realize beforehand; foresee

Ⅱ. Read the following text and fill in the blanks with the words given in the box.

| restructure | empower | drawback | corrode | encourage |
| mortgage | vicious | hangover | foreclosure | bankruptcy |

A broader set of policies could help to work off the (1) _____ faster. One priority is to (2) _____ more write-downs of mortgage debt. Almost a quarter of all Americans with (3) _____ owe more than their houses are worth. Until that changes the (4) _____ cycle of rising (5) _____ and falling prices will continue. There are plenty of ideas on offer, from changing the (6) _____ law so that judges can (7) _____ mortgage debt to (8) _____ special trustees to write down loans. They all have (9) _____, but a fetid pool of underwater mortgages will, much like Japan's loans to zombie firms, (10) _____ the financial system and harm the recovery.

Text B Training Needs Assessment: A Must for Developing an Effective Training Program

> **导读：** 培训是一种有组织的知识传递、技能传递、标准传递、信息传递、信念传递、管理训诫行为。为了达到统一的科学技术规范、标准化作业，通过目标规划设定、知识和信息传递、技能熟练演练、作业达成评测、结果交流公告等现代信息化的流程，让员工通过一定的教育训练技术手段，达到预期提高水平的目标。而影响培训效果至关重要的环节便是前期的培训评估，它统领整个培训项目的框架，决定培训的目标、方法、实施步骤等各个方面。

Training needs assessment is an ongoing process of gathering data to determine what training needs exist so that training can be developed to help the organization accomplish its objectives. Conducting needs assessment is fundamental to the success of a training program. Often, organizations will develop and implement training without first conducting a needs analysis. These organizations run the risk of overdoing training, doing too little training, or missing the point completely.

There are four main reasons why needs analysis must be done before training programs are developed.

(1) To identify specific problem areas in the organization. HR and management must know what the problems are so that the most appropriate training (if training is the answer) will be directed to those organizational problems. For example, if a manager approached the HR department with a request for a communications program, too often the trainer's

response (eager to serve management) will be to proceed to look around for a good communications program and conduct training without conducting a needs assessment first. This approach will inevitably fail. Nodding their heads appreciatively, everyone says "That was a good program," but when they go back to their departments, work proceeds as usual because the training was not directed to the real needs of the participants. The proper response should have been, "Yes, but let us start by taking a look at the situation. We will talk to a few people to find out what the problems are. Then when we develop the program, we can zero in on a specific situation rather than just use a random approach."

(2) **To obtain management support.** Management usually thinks training is a "nice thing to do." This stance can be laid directly at the doorstep of a poor (or nonexistent) needs assessment. The way to obtain management support is to make certain that the training directly affects what happens in that manager's department. Trainers should view themselves the same way that management does, making a direct contribution to the bottom line. Management will be committed to training when HR can show that it clearly improves performance on the job. As a result, training programs and budgets will not be the first things cut or trimmed.

(3) **To develop data for evaluation.** Unless informational needs are developed prior to conducting training, the evaluations that take place after the program may not be valid. In conducting a needs analysis first, trainers can measure the effectiveness of a program.

(4) **To determine the costs and benefits of training.** Training is usually looked upon as a nuisance rather than a contribution to the bottom line of the organization. This happens when trainers fail to develop a cost-benefit analysis for the training they conduct. Few managers would balk at spending $20,000 to correct a problem costing them $200,000 a year. Yet, most of the time trainers complain that management will not spend money on training. However, a thorough needs assessment that identifies the problems and performance deficiencies, allows management to put a cost factor on the training needs.

The major question trainers need to address in cost-benefit analysis is, "What is the difference between the cost of no training versus the cost of training?" This entails finding out what the costs (out-of-pocket, salary, lost productivity, etc.) would be if the need continues without being met. Next, an analysis must be made of the cost of conducting the training program that can change the situation. The difference between these two factors will usually tell both the trainer and manager whether or not the training should be conducted.

Human Resources (HR) professionals and line managers also need to be aware that training is not the "cure all" for organizational problems. Neither should it be used as a tool to reward excellent performance, or as motivation to correct poor performance. The purpose of training is to support the achievement of organizational goals by increasing the necessary skills of its employees.

Training is appropriate when your organization can expect to gain more benefit from the training than it invested in its cost. The value of any training investment to the organization must rely on the vision and judgment of line supervisors and managers. You may authorize training to build skills and knowledge levels that help employees contribute to your organizational mission(s) better. In some cases, the need is immediate and the training remedial; in other cases, the aim is to update and maintain professional knowledge; and in still others, the goal is to prepare for requirements anticipated by higher level officials.

The following factors might indicate training or development needs of your employees:

A. Development of employee/management skills to fill a current need
- Trainee or intern training plans
- Reduction in Force (RIF) placements
- New Employees
- New supervisors
- Managerial competency assessments
- Reassignments
- Promotions

B. Employee relations/organizational problems
- Performance problems
- Production problems
- Safety problems
- Inspection deficiencies

C. Meet changing needs
- New technology
- New equipment or programs
- Modernization of equipment
- Mission changes
- Laws and regulations

D. Career development
- Employees' requests
- Career enhancement plans

The Purpose and Objective for Conducting Needs Assessment

Identifying training needs for your employees requires careful scrutiny of mission objectives, personnel, production, raw materials, costs, and other factors. The training requirements you identify factor into the total training budget forecasted for your organization and your installation, and impact the amount of funds that are allocated by senior management.

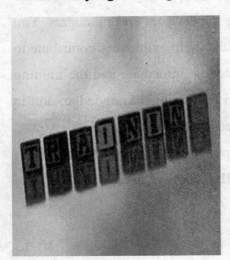

Conducting a needs assessment is useful in identifying:

- Organizational goals and its effectiveness in achieving these goals.
- Gaps or discrepancies between employee skills and the skills required for effective job performance.
- Problems that may not be solved by training. If policies, practices, and procedures need to be corrected or adjusted, this is a concern for top management, not a training concern.
- Conditions under which the training and development activity will occur.

In addition to providing a clear direction for identifying training needs, a needs analysis also serves as a basis for evaluating the effectiveness of the training program. Upon completion of the analysis, you have a basis for comparison. In the absence of a needs analysis, training results are usually subjective and might not be attributable to the training.

Implementing and developing training programs can be expensive, so it makes sense to analyze training needs at the onset so that training can be tailored to focus on specific needs and withstand evaluation after training.

Conducting a Needs Analysis

In selecting which training needs analysis techniques to use, one requires answers to questions such as the following:

1. What is the nature of the problem being addressed by instruction?
2. How have training needs been identified in the past and with what results?
3. What is the budget for the analysis?
4. How is training needs analysis perceived in the organization?
5. Who is available to help conduct the training needs analysis?
6. What are the timeframes for completing the exercise?
7. What will be the measure of a successful training needs analysis report?

The time spent and the degree of formality will differ according to particular needs and the organization involved. There are, however, four basic steps:

1. Gather data to identify needs

This can be accomplished through:
- Surveys/Questionnaires
- Interviews
- Performance appraisals
- Observations
- Tests
- Assessment centers
- Focus groups
- Document reviews
- Advisory committees

Each method has special characteristics that can affect both the kind and quality of the information obtained. For instance, an interview can reflect the interviewer's bias, while a questionnaire can have sampling bias if only a few participants return the survey. It is best to use more than one method to help validate the data, as you can get different types of information from the different methods. For example, you can use questionnaires to gather facts and utilize follow-up interviews to delve more into why people answered questions the way they did.

It is also important to include persons from a cross-section of the target employees for training. Sample people with varying experience levels or you will not have a valid sample, and training will only be effective for a certain part of the total population you targeted.

2. Determine what needs can be met by training and development

If there is indication of performance deficiency, the next step is to determine what needs can be met by training and development. If the problems relate to employee relations such as poor morale, lack of motivation, or inability to learn, training is not a solution. Human resources professionals who use training as a motivator misunderstand the purpose of training, which is simply to pass on missing skills and knowledge to employees who are willing and able to learn. Problems arising from non-training issues such as insufficient rewards or obsolete equipment can be identified and referred to management.

3. Proposing solutions

After determining that training is a potential solution, HR professionals will need to closely examine if formal training is the best way to meet the need. You might find that practice or feedback is all that is needed.

- Practice is useful if a particular skill was taught but not used. For example, an employee might be trained in all aspects of a word processing program but use only a small portion of those skills. If the job requires expansion of those skills, the employee may need time to review additional word processing material and practice using them.

- Feedback to employees concerning their work is critical in maintaining quality. Managers and supervisors need to periodically evaluate job performance and tell employees what they are doing correctly or incorrectly to avoid work skills diminishing. If an employee was not able to perform a certain skill, using an existing program to retrain or designing a new program may be the appropriate solution.

4. Identifying the next step

Once needs have been analyzed and identified, the next step is to develop the training proposal itself. It should spell out the need for training, the expected results, the people to be trained, and the expected consequences if training is not conducted. A key decision is whether to use an existing program or design a new training program.

We have seen that the rationale for developing a training program relies heavily on identifying training needs, and justifying the costs and benefits to the organization. Without a clear understanding of needs, training efforts are at best randomly useful and at worst, useless. The trainer will only be successful and perceived as such to the extent that needs are carefully assessed, and programs developed and carried out that meet those needs. The end result is a more precise picture of training needs, which can lead to a performance improvement oriented training program and better results from training.

Notes:

1. Reduction in Force（RIF）（强制裁员）: Reduction in Force also called redundancy in the UK, is the temporary suspension or permanent termination of employment of an employee or (more commonly) a group of employees for business reasons, such as when certain positions are no longer necessary or when a business slow-down occurs. Originally the term referred exclusively to a temporary interruption in work, as when factory work cyclically falls off. The term however nowadays usually means the permanent elimination of a position, requiring the addition of "temporary" to specify the original meaning.

2. Bottom Line: Bottom line refers to a company's net earnings, net income or earnings per share (EPS). The reference to "bottom" describes the relative location of the net income figure on a company's income statement. Most companies aim to improve their bottom lines through two simultaneous methods: growing revenues (i.e., generate top-line growth) and increasing efficiency (or cutting costs).

Words & Expressions:

1. zero in   调整归零；瞄准具校正
2. stance [stæns] n. 立场；姿态；位置；准备击球姿势

3. trim [trim] vt. 修剪；整理；装点
   vi. 削减
   n. 修剪；整齐；情形
   adj. 整齐的
4. valid ['vælid] adj. 有效的，有根据的；正当的
5. nuisance ['nju:səns] n. 讨厌的人；损害；麻烦事；讨厌的东西
6. balk at　回避，畏缩
7. deficiency [di'fiʃənsi] n. 缺陷，缺点；缺乏；不足的数额
8. entail [in'teil] vt. 必需，使承担；[律]限定继承
   n. 限定继承，限定继承权；限定继承的财产
9. remedial [ri'mi:diəl] adj. 治疗的；补救的；矫正的
10. intern [in'tə:n] n. 实习生，实习医师
    vt. 拘留，软禁
    vi. 作实习医师
11. inspection [in'spekʃən] n. 视察，检查
12. scrutiny ['skru:tini] n. 详细审查；监视；细看；选票复查
13. forecast ['fɔ:kɑ:st] vt. 预报，预测；预示
    n. 预测，预报；预想
    vi. 进行预报，作预测
14. installation [ˌinstə'leiʃən] n. 安装，装置；就职
15. allocate ['æləukeit] vt. 分配；拨出；使坐落于
    vi. 分配；指定
16. discrepancy [dis'krepənsi] n. 不符；矛盾；相差
17. attributable [ə'tribjutəbl] adj. 可归于……的；可归属的
18. onset ['ɔnset] n. 开始，着手；发作；攻击，进攻
19. formality [fɔ:'mæliti] n. 礼节；拘谨；仪式；正式手续
20. appraisal [ə'preizəl] n. 评价；估价（尤指估价财产，以便征税）；估计
21. validate ['vælideit] vt. 证实，验证；确认；使生效
22. obsolete ['ɔbsəli:t] adj. 废弃的；老式的
    n. 废词；陈腐的人
    vt. 淘汰；废弃
23. diminish [di'miniʃ] vt. 使减少；使变小
    vi. 减少，缩小；变小

Exercises:

I. Fill in the blanks with the suitable words given in the box. Change the form when necessary.

| discrepancy | entail | diminish | validate | appraisal |
| scrutiny | deficiency | allocate | stance | forecast |

1. We could not reconsider our policy unless they indicated new flexibility in its negotiating _____.
2. Memory loss is caused by lack of oxygen to the brain and nutrition _____.
3. Hence, modernization in China remains a long and uphill journey that will _____ many years of work.
4. Candidates for public office submit their platforms, or programs, to the voters for their _____ and approval.
5. He was left with egg all over his face when his _____ was proved wrong.
6. People usually express their interests by what they habitually talk about and how they _____ their time and money.
7. The conception of design has its aesthetic features concerning culture, interaction, _____ and form.
8. To carry out teaching _____ reasonably and provide the education quality of teaching the effective guarantee.
9. In order to _____ the agreement between yourself and your employer, you must both sign it.
10. As the size of civil financing increases, the comparative advantage on trading cost will gradually _____ or even disappear.

II. Decide whether the following statements are true (T) or false (F) according to the passage.

1. When everyone says "That was a good program", it means that this is a fruitful

training program. (   )

2. Only when HR can demonstrate that trainging may improve efficiency on employees' jobs, the management will support training and not cut the budget of training program. (   )

3. The purpose of training is to reward excellent performance and to cure all for organizational problems. (   )

4. Different organizations and particular needs lead to different time spent and the degree of formality of training program. (   )

5. Trainers will have a valid sample when people come from a fixed section of the target employees for training. (   )

Ⅲ. Translate the following sentences into Chinese.

1. Training needs assessment is an ongoing process of gathering data to determine what training needs exist so that training can be developed to help the organization accomplish its objectives.

2. In some cases, the need is immediate and the training remedial; in other cases, the aim is to update and maintain professional knowledge; and in still others, the goal is to prepare for requirements anticipated by higher level officials.

3. The training requirements you identify factor into the total training budget forecasted for your organization and your installation, and impact the amount of funds that are allocated by senior management.

4. Implementing and developing training programs can be expensive, so it makes sense to analyze training needs at the onset so that training can be tailored to focus on specific needs and withstand evaluation after training.

5. Managers and supervisors need to periodically evaluate job performance and tell employees what they are doing correctly or incorrectly to avoid work skills diminishing.

> **Supplementary Reading**

An Innovative Method for Role-specific Quality-training Evaluation

How well an organisation has promulgated and implemented quality practices throughout the organisation is to a large extent dependent on the effectiveness of the organisation's quality-training programme for employees. This premise is supported by a significant body of literature that explores the critical role played by quality-training programmes in establishing a total quality management (TQM) infrastructure in an organisation. Oppenheim states that transformation (of companies) to total quality requires changes in paradigms and culture by all employees. This does not come naturally and, therefore, requires adequate training of all employees. Kanji has argued that training in TQM should be used to change the culture of the people. Tollinson has indicated that introducing TQM calls for a training strategy that integrates training, basic skills improvement and job skills, since they are interdependent. It is interesting to note that, in the software industry in particular, one of the two primary causes for most software development project failures is lack of employee training, especially in quality assurance.

A sound quality-training prog ramme is the vehicle that ensures that all employees are adequately qualified to perform their jobs in accordance with applicable quality requirements. It follows that, an effective quality-training programme is one that adequately addresses the varied training needs of employees in

different roles in the organisation. This requires that two critical elements be part of the organisation's training programmean assessment of quality-training needs of employees, and an evaluation of the quality-training to ascertain whether or not the identified training needs have been met. Therefore, prior to developing quality-training material and conducting quality-training, a training needs assessment should be performed. Minimally, this includes employees that are within the scope of the organisation's quality management system, such as requirements engineers, product managers, software engineers, software testers, quality assurance personnel, configuration management personnel, customer support personnel, and so on. The identified quality-training needs them to serve as the set of objectives for the development of quality-training material, and later serve as a basis for evaluating the effectiveness of the quality-training after delivery to the target audience.

Training needs assessment typically entails examining training needs at three levels: organisational level, task (or role-specific) level, and individual level. Training needs assessment at the organisational level entails examination of where training is needed in the organisation and under what conditions the training will be conducted. It identifies the knowledge, skills and abilities that employees will need for the future, as the organisation and their jobs evolve or change. Training needs assessment at the task level begins with job requirements and compares employee knowledge and skills to determine training needs. Examining job descriptions and specifications provides necessary information on expected performance and the skills employees need to accomplish their work. Training needs assessment at the individual level targets individual employees and how they perform in their jobs. Using information or data from an employee's performance review in determining training programme needs is the most common method. If an employee's review reveals deficiencies, training can be designed to help the employee meet the performance standard.

Once required training has been developed and delivered to address the training needs identified from the training needs assessment, it is followed by a training evaluation. Training evaluation is the process of assessing the results or outcomes of training. It loops back to training needs assessment to determine how much and how well the training that was delivered solved the identified performance problems linked to knowledge or skills deficiencies. Many training evaluation models are in use in the industry; however, the model that is the most widely adopted was first proposed by Kirkpatrick in 1959. Kirkpatrick's training evaluation framework comprises four levels at which training can be evaluated:

- Level 1 Evaluation: Reactions—focuses on participants' reactions to the training; this includes feedback on the instructor, food, facilities, training material, and so on;
- Level 2 Evaluation: Learning—focuses on learning, which may be a combination of knowledge, skills or attitude acquisition;
- Level 3 Evaluation: Behaviour change—focuses on behaviour change; specifically, it evaluates how much or how well the participants applied what they learned upon returning to

their jobs; and

• **Level 4 Evaluation: Results**—focuses on results, that is, how the training translates to bottom-line results, such as productivity improvements, defects reduction, and so on.

1. Essential elements of a quality-training programme

Having recognised the value of establishing a sound quality-training programme, how does an organisation go about establishing such a programme? The answer to the question entails determining what should be the key elements of such a quality-training programme.

• **Assess training needs:** This entails identifying employee training needs and recording them in an employee training plan (or other equivalent means).

• **Prepare the training material (if required):** If the training method requires the training to be delivered by means of a formal presentation or if it involves use of training material, then required training material should be developed.

• **Conduct the training:** Conduct the training as per the specified training method in the employee training plans. The training may be performed internally or by an external vendor.

• **Perform training evaluation:** Perform role-specific training evaluation to verify that the training was effective and adequate. Take appropriate corrective actions as needed to address the noted deficiencies in the training. This may entail improving the training material, method of delivery, or identifying additional training for the employee.

• **Maintain employee training plans:** The training plans once created should be maintained to record the trainings completed. Furthermore, the determination of employee training needs is done not only at the time of hiring the employee but also on an ongoing basis. This necessitates ongoing maintenance of employee training plans to record new training needs.

2. Identifying and recording role-specific quality-training needs

The purpose of an employee training plan is to document the identified training needs to qualify an employee to perform his or her job. This is done by creating training plans for the various roles in an organisation, and for each role, specifying the required training along with the training methods and training completion criteria. Additionally, if required, the training vendor may also be identified. A sample employee training plan is shown in the following Table.

Training needs assessment, including assessment of quality-training needs, may be performed by using various techniques, such as employee interviews, onsite observations, focus groups and survey questionnaires (e. g. employee opinion surveys). Employee training needs may be identified at the time of: promotion or transfer of the employee; employee performance review; and new product release or major revision of an existing product that necessitates new training for employees. Training needs may also be determined during the course of everyday process execution. For example, deficiencies in employee competencies may surface during quality audits; a change in a process may result in need for retraining of employees; and a breakdown in process execution attributed to human failure may result in a need for retraining of employees.

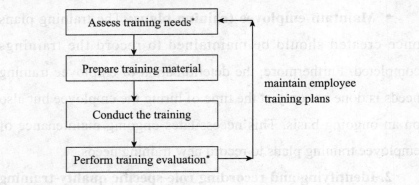

Once the completion criteria for training as identified in the employee training plan have been satisfactorily met, the training can be considered complete and the employee training plan updated accordingly. Note that, in effect, the employee training plan may thus serve as the training record as well (supplemented of course with records such as any course completion certificates, marked quizzes, attendance records and so on).

Tips

培训方法分类：

- 微笑式培训(smile training)：以人为中心，通过各种特殊事件、富有激情的演讲，以及对参与者进行表扬，让受训者觉得培训过程非常有趣。
- 上手培训(hands-on training)：新员工首先对自己以后需要执行的工作进行观察，然后，通过长时间与那些经验丰富的师傅或同事们在一起工作，达到消化、吸收和掌握各种技能的目的。
- 工具式培训(instrument training)：通过标准化的、没有为组织或组织中的工作量身定做的评价工具，获得与自己技能有关的知识和信息。
- 以学习目标为基础的培训(objective-based instruction)：包括结构化的、指导性的培训设计，关注的焦点在于为了更好地执行某一任务，任职者必须学习哪些具体的知识和技能。

● 企业内训 (corporate training)：通过请培训师给员工进行系列的培训。

● 公开课程 (open courses)：参加短期的培训课程，企业可以派送相关岗位的人员去学习相关的短期课程，既节省企业的培训成本又使人因岗位不同更好地接受培训。

Unit 10

Corporate Culture

Text A What Is Corporate Culture?

> **导读**：企业文化，即企业个性，是一个组织由其价值观、信念、仪式、符号、处事方式等组成的其特有的文化形象，具体指企业全体员工在企业运行过程中所培育形成的、与企业组织行为相关联的、并事实上成为全体员工主流意识而被共同遵守的最高目标、价值体系、基本信念及企业组织行为规范的总和。企业文化集中反映了企业的关键价值，是企业的灵魂，是推动企业发展的不竭动力。企业文化既有有形部分，也有无形部分。

In today's radically changed business climate, corporate culture is a key component in the success of today's business organizations. After years of failed fads, such as outsourcing, downsizing, flawed go-for-growth strategies, business-process reengineering, and outrageous cases of corporate lawlessness, it is believed that corporate culture is most critical to the success and very survival of today's corporation.

What Is Corporate Culture? Corporate culture or organizational culture is an idea in the field of organizational studies and management which describes the psychology, attitudes, experiences, beliefs and values (personal and cultural values) of an organization. Also it is called as "beliefs and ideas about what kinds of goals members of an organization should pursue and ideas about the appropriate kinds or standards of behavior organizational members should use to achieve these goals."

Typologies of organizational cultures. Several methods have been used to classify organizational culture. Here is a typology of organizational culture described by Hofstede. Hofstede looked for national differences between over 100,000 of IBM's employees in different parts of the world, in an attempt to find aspects of culture that might influence business behavior. Hofstede identified four dimensions of culture in his study of national influences.

• Power distance—The degree to which a society expects there to be differences in the levels of power. A high score suggests that there is an expectation that some individuals wield larger amounts of power than others. A low score reflects the view that all people should have equal rights.

• Uncertainty avoidance—reflects the extent to which a society accepts uncertainty and risk.

• Individualism vs. collectivism—individualism is contrasted with collectivism, and refers to the extent to which people are expected to stand up for themselves, or alternatively act predominantly as a member of the group or organization. However, recent researches have shown that high individualism may not necessarily mean low collectivism, and vice versa. Research indicates that the two concepts are actually unrelated. Some people and cultures might have both high individualism and high collectivism, for example. Someone who highly values duty to his or her group does not necessarily give a low priority to personal freedom and self-sufficiency.

• Masculinity vs. femininity—refers to the value placed on traditionally male or female values. Male values for example include competitiveness, assertiveness, ambition, and the accumulation of wealth and material possessions.

How about corporate culture in today's corporation?

IBM exec: Culture is your company's No. 1 asset Culture. Now that's a subject that most leaders would be wise to pay more attention to. Ginny Rometty is speaking at an IBM event. One boss who does: Ginny Rometty at IBM. And to her benefit. Currently in charge of sales and marketing and strategy at Big Blue—and No. 8 on Fortune's Most Powerful Women list—Rometty is mentioned in Fortune's current cover story about IBM as a possible successor to CEO Sam Palmisano.

Recently Rometty spoke about culture at the Yale CEO Summit. Her talk to be so good that it's worth my sharing a few of her points here. Culture, Rometty told the audience, has become the defining issue that will distinguish the most successful businesses from the rest of the pack. For instance, Ford got back on track by rerouting its culture. CEO Alan Mulally rallied faithful followers. And in turn, the entire organization refocused on Ford's core value: quality. The biggest cultural challenge for corporate leaders: social media. Rometty cited Nielsen research that shows social media accounts for almost a quarter of the time Americans spend online. Social media's consumption of time spent on mobile devices? Around 50%.

So, she said, "Your message has to be a dialogue, and it has to be authentic." Especially, she added, since some research suggests that consumers trust information from each other twelve times more than they trust messages or ads from companies. Most importantly, "You have to rethink the way you treat and talk to employees," she added. On Facebook, Rometty said, more people "self-identify" with IBM than with any other organization. Given this reality, IBM decided to cede control to its employees—that is, let them devise behavior guidelines. This process began in 2005, when IBM employees used a wiki to create a set of guidelines for all IBMers who wanted to blog. Since then, IBMers have evolved the guidelines to include all social media.

Today, IBM's "Social Computing Guidelines" aren't necessarily what would come out of an Office of the President. For example, No. 10 of 12 on the list is: "Don't pick fights, be the first to correct your mistakes."

Hey, it works. This sort of culture-carrying throughout the organization has helped propel IBM near the top of Fortune's Most Admired Companies list. And it has helped propel Rometty's career as well. Now that she's close to the top, she believes more than ever: "Culture has to come from the bottom up."

The role that corporate culture plays in other top companies. Here are other top companies that are the most admired for their ability to attract and keep talented people.

1. Apple

Even beyond visionary leader Steve Jobs, Apple is brimming with talent. One reassuring star: Tim Cook, the chief operating officer who has been able to step in as No. 1 during Jobs' health battles. Cook sits on the board of Nike, where his expertise in global sales and operations is valued. A graduate of Duke University, he's held leadership jobs at companies including Compaq and IBM. Then there's Jonathan Ive, senior VP of industrial design. Ive was named Designer of the Year by the Design Museum London in 2003 and is regarded as leader of one of the world's best design teams.

2. Google

Google, long a magnet for tech whizzes, has been losing valued employees lately to rivals like Facebook. As part of its renewed quest to attract and retain the best talent, the company says this will be one of its biggest hiring years ever. Of course, Google already is renowned for showering employees with perks like free laundry and free food at its Mountain View, Calif., headquarters. And it caters to many disciplines. As Senior VP of Engineering and Research Alan Eustace puts it, "there's something at Google for everyone—from geo, to enterprise, to video."

3. Procter & Gamble

P&G is a strong believer in building from within, and the proof is at the top. Five members of the executive team—including CEO Bob McDonald and several vice chairmen—joined the company as entry-level employees in the 70s'. Big talent rarely leaves to seek green pastures, but the people who do tend to leave for high profile jobs. Among them are Meg Whitman, former CEO of eBay; Jim McNerney, President and CEO of

Boeing, and Jeffrey Immelt, Chairman and CEO of GE.

4. Walt Disney

Disney is famed for its animated talent—from Mickey Mouse to Prince of Persia. But the entertainment giant also is renowned for its corporate talent. "We have a deep bench," CEO Robert Iger wrote in the company's 2010 annual report, "but we also look to the outside to make sure we have new perspectives and the right expertise in a media environment where conditions are changing constantly." The company's acquisitions, which include Pixar and Marvel, "add to our ranks of talented artists, engineers, and business innovators," Iger said.

5. Nestlé

The great minds behind Kit Kat bars aren't just focused on chocolate lovers. Nestlé employs more than 5,000 people at 29 research, development and technology facilities worldwide to help make the company's products nutritious and enjoyable all in the same bite.

Its Dreyer's Slow Churned flavors, for example, are half the fat of regular ice cream. After acquiring Jenny Craig in 2006, it launched "Jenny's Cuisines" for weight management.

Company scientists and nutritionists work hand in hand to churn out items that are healthy, nutritional and innovative (peelable ice cream, anyone?) as part of its "Good Food, Good Life" mission.

Nestlé also operates research centers around the world that may bring in expertise from business partners, universities, and independent institutes. Its new innovation center in Switzerland, for example, focuses on cereal, and runs as part of a joint venture with General Mills. Simply put, Nestlé looks far and wide for genius—in science and in food.

6. Royal Dutch Shell

Shell USA's workforce is in the midst of a culture shift. As many baby boomers approach retirement age, the global oil company has launched several programs to attract new talent to the energy industry. For example, Shell runs a one-week residential engineering camp to train top engineering students in the U.S. The company also offers technology internships for local community college and technical school students.

Notes:

1. **IBM** (**International Business Machines**（国际商业机器公司）): is an American multinational technology and consulting firm headquartered in Armonk, New York. IBM manufactures and sells computer hardware and software, and it offers infrastructure, hosting and consulting services in areas ranging from mainframe computers to nanotechnology. In 2010, IBM was ranked the 20th largest firm in the U. S. by *Fortune* and the 33rd largest globally by *Forbes*. Other rankings that year include company for leaders (*Fortune*), best global brand (*Interbrand*), green company (*Newsweek*), most admired company (*Fortune*), and most innovative company (*Fast Company*).

2. **Apple Inc.**（苹果公司）: is an American multinational corporation that designs and markets consumer electronics, computer software, and personal computers. The company's best-known hardware products include the Macintosh line of computers, the iPod, the iPhone and the iPad.

3. **Procter & Gamble Co.**（宝洁公司）: is a Fortune 500 American multinational corporation headquartered in Downtown Cincinnati, Ohio that manufactures a wide range of consumer goods. It is 6th in Fortune's Most Admired Companies 2010 list. P&G is credited with many business innovations including brand management and the soap opera.

4. **Nestlé S. A.**（雀巢公司）: is one of the largest food and nutrition companies in the world, founded and headquartered in Vevey, Switzerland. Today, the company operates in 86 countries around the world.

5. **Royal Dutch Shell**（荷兰皇家壳牌集团）: is a global oil and gas company headquartered in The Hague, Netherlands and with its registered office at the Shell Centre in London, United Kingdom. It is the largest energy company and the second-largest company in the world measured by revenues and is one of the six oil and gas "supermajors".

Words & Expressions:

1. outsourcing [ˈaut,sɔːsiŋ] n. 外包；外购；外部采办
2. downsizing [ˈdaun,saiziŋ] n. 精简，裁员；缩小规模
3. dimension [diˈmenʃən] n. 维；尺寸；次元；容积
   vt. 标出尺寸
   adj. 规格的
4. wield [wiːld] vt. 使用；行使；挥舞
5. exec [egˈzek] n. 执行，执行程序；主任参谋，副舰长
   abbr. 实行 (execute)；实行的 (executive)
6. reroute [riːˈruːt] vt. 变更旅程；按新的特定路线运送
7. rally [ˈræli] vi. 团结；重整；恢复；（网球等）连续对打
   vt. 团结；集合；恢复健康、力量等
   n. 集会；回复；公路赛车会
8. account for 占……比例
9. authentic [ɔːˈθentik] adj. 真正的，真实的；可信的
10. cede [siːd] vt. 放弃；割让（领土）
11. propel [prəˈpel] vt. 推进；驱使；激励；驱策
12. visionary [ˈviʒənəri] adj. 梦想的；幻影的
    n. 空想家；梦想者；有眼力的人
13. brim with 洋溢着；充满着
14. whizz [hwiz] n. 专家；精明的人；子弹等在空中掠过的声音（等于 whiz）
    vt. 飕飕作声（等于 whiz）
15. internship [ˈintəːnʃip] n.（美）实习期；实习医师职位；实习生
16. high profile [ˈprəufail] 鲜明的姿态；引人注目的高姿态；明确的立场
17. acquisition [ˌækwiˈziʃən] n. 兼并，购并；获得，所获之物
18. churn [tʃəːn] out 艰苦地做出；大量炮制
19. baby boomer 婴儿潮时代出生的人
20. far and wide adv. 广泛地；到处

Exercises:

I. Fill in the blanks with the suitable words given in the box. Change the form when necessary.

| propel | cede | churn out | whizz | acquisitions | wield |

1. Most of our real estate exposure is institutional _____ of office buildings—largely in major markets—central business districts.
2. LeBlanc thinks the President's visibility with the Volt will _____ GM to more profitability.
3. Some pulp writers _____ two or three short stories a day.
4. Trains _____ through the station by the village on their way to London every day.
5. She admits to having trouble with some of the big guns her character has to _____.
6. In an attempt to show they are serious about supporting a solution to the protracted Cyprus problem, Britain has renewed an offer to _____ about half the territory of its bases in Cyprus.

II. Decide whether the following statements are true (T) or false (F) according to the passage.

1. Corporate culture refers to beliefs and ideas about what kinds of goals that only the top members of an organization should pursue. (   )
2. According to Hofstede's study of national influences, the following all belong to dimensions of culture: *power distance, uncertainty avoidance, masculinity vs. femininity and individualism vs. collectivism.* (   )
3. Ginny Rometty currently in charge of sales and marketing and strategy at Big Blue ranked as No. 8 on Fortune's Most Powerful Women list. (   )
4. The article mentions six companies that pay great attention to corporater culture in total. (   )
5. In Nestlé company scientists and nutritionists work individually to churn out items

that are healthy, nutritional and innovative as part of its "Good Food, Good Life" mission. ( )

Text B Four Steps to Go Green Like eBay
—Starting with Employees

> **导读**：团队精神是大局意识、协作精神和服务精神的集中体现。团队精神的基础是尊重个人的兴趣和成就，核心是协同合作，最高境界是全体成员的向心力、凝聚力，它主张挥洒个性、表现特长，保证了成员共同完成任务目标，而明确的协作意愿和协作方式则产生了真正的内心动力。团队精神具有目标导向功能、凝聚功能、激励功能和控制功能，可以说，团队是一种精神，是一种力量，是现代企业文化中不可缺少的！

In a recent interview, Annie Lesroart of eBay, shared with us how eBay implemented a fast, ambitious and effective strategy to go green. From forty employees, the program expanded to hundreds of thousands of eBay buyers and sellers (including people who don't even work at eBay!)

How did this happen? And how can it happen for you?

The change began over pizza and soda. A group of employees from a company known for its innovation and leadership could not help but notice the irony of the styrofoam cups in their hands. Turns out that styrofoam constitutes as much as 30% of landfills worldwide. A discussion ensued around what it means to be green, each of the employees deciding something had to be done. Without approval, mission or mandate, and with very modest ambitions, these employees formed the "Green Team."

Their first endeavor? Eliminate styrofoam cups from the break room

From this modest beginning, the eBay Green Team has grown to include more than 2 300 employees in 23 countries. As a recent judge on a panel for the 2010 Just Means Social Innovation Award, I had the privilege of reviewing the eBay Green Team's application. Not surprisingly, the Green Team won the award for "Best Employee Engagement Strategy" — and shows no signs of slowing down. Take a look at the website to see just how impressive their work is: *http://www.ebaygreenteam.com/green-at-ebay*.

Recently, at the Ceres 2010 conference in Boston, I enjoyed a fascinating conversation with eBay's Annie Lescroart about the project. She outlined four key steps that enabled the eBay Green Team to succeed. I recommend these steps to any group of employees wanting to see their company become more green and sustainable.

Just Do It

The group of forty employees who decided to take action didn't wait for permission. They determined the steps that could demonstrate their easy ability to go green and allowed the program to grow itself.

Look for Quick and Easy Wins

Lescroart said that after a handful of initial successful projects, the company was open to bigger projects. Recently, with the leadership of the eBay Green Team, eBay has constructed the largest solar panel in San Jose, CA. It is San Jose's largest with some 3,248 panels.

Make the Business Case

At some point, the Green Team needed to demonstrate that going green and buying solar panels made business sense. At that stage, the executive level leadership was able to support the effort and fund the program with proof in hand. And remember it's far more convincing when you make the case on both an emotional and rational level. Using only numbers won't convince anyone to change; using only a great story won't offer clear direction. You need both. For more about how to help change happen, read Switch.

Tie It to Core Values

eBay prides itself on innovation and creativity. The company also has a strong sense of the inherent "goodness" of their people and the need to allow everyone in the company to contribute in meaningful ways. The Green Team built their approach utilizing these values and before long the CEO was challenging all 15,000 employees to submit more ideas on how to make eBay a greater company.

The Outcome So Far Has Been Pretty Substantial

8,200 lbs of e-waste collected at SJ e-recycling drive in May 2009.

Employees in North America rode over 3,500 miles during Bike to Work Week in May 2009.

650 kW San Jose solar array takes 18% of our energy consumption at that campus off the grid; green building features at same site deliver energy savings of approx. 39%, smart irrigation system expected to save at least 8 million gallons of water, or 25%–30% of the building's irrigation needs—all innovations and impacts directly attributable to Green Team actions.

Supporting a Net Metering bill that was signed into law in Utah; the bill allows businesses and residences to sell excess power generated from reusable resources back to the local utility.

In addition, the eBay Green Team has looked for ways to influence their community of buyers and sellers (over 90 million strong) towards similar activities. One key strategy has been social media. Utilizing Facebook (3,079 fans), Twitter (3,000 followers) and, of course, eBay (110,000 Green Team members), the message to "buy, sell and think green every day" continues to gain momentum.

Notes：

1. **eBay Inc.**（易趣）: is an American Internet company that manages eBay.com, an online auction and shopping website in which people and businesses buy and sell a broad variety of goods and services worldwide. Founded in 1995, eBay is one of the notable success stories of the dot-com bubble; it is now a multi-billion dollar business with operations localized in over thirty countries.

2. **San Jose**（圣何塞，美国加州西部城市）: Silicon valley city San Jose is located in silicon valley high-tech capital.

3. **Going green**（绿色环保化）: Basically, going green means to live life, as an individual as well as a community, in a way that is friendly to the natural environmental and is sustainable for the earth. It means contributing towards maintaining the natural ecological balance in the environment, and preserving the planet and its natural systems and resources. It also means taking steps, whether big or small, to minimize the harm you do to the environment (including the carbon footprints you leave behind), as a result of inhabiting this planet.

4. **FaceBook**（脸谱网）: is a social network service and website launched in February 2004, operated and privately owned by Facebook, Inc. As of January 2011, Facebook has more than 600 million active users. Users may create a personal profile, add other users as friends, and exchange messages, including automatic notifications when they update their profile.

5. **Twitter**（微博）: is a website, owned and operated by Twitter Inc., which offers a social networking and microblogging service, enabling its users to send and read messages called *tweets*. Tweets are text-based posts of up to 140 characters displayed on the user's profile page.

Words & Expressions:

1. styrofoam ['stairəfəum] n. 泡沫聚苯乙烯
2. landfill ['lændfil] n. 垃圾填埋地；垃圾堆
3. constitute ['kɔnstitjuːt] vt. 组成，构成；建立；任命
4. mandate ['mændeit] n. 授权；命令，指令；委托管理
   vt. 授权；托管
5. endeavor [in'devə] n. 努力；尽力（等于 endeavour）
   vt./vi. 努力；尽力

6. sustainable [sə'steinəbl] *adj.* 可以忍受的；足可支撑的；养得起的
7. initial [i'niʃəl] *adj.* 最初的；字首的
   vt. 用姓名的首字母签名
   n. 词首大写字母
8. solar panel   太阳电池板
9. utilize ['ju:tilaiz] *vt.* 利用
10. submit [səb'mit] *vt.* 使服从；主张；呈递
    vi. 提交；服从
11. e-waste   *n.* 电子垃圾
12. solar array   太阳能电池阵；太阳电池板；太阳组
13. utility [ju:'tiləti] *n.* 实用；效用；公共设施；功用
    adj. 实用的；通用的；有多种用途的
14. momentum [məu'mentəm] *n.* 势头；[物] 动量；动力；冲力

Exercises:

I. **Fill in the blanks with the suitable words given in the box. Change the form when necessary.**

sustain   constitute   endeavor   mandate   attribute to   submit

1. She said the commission will _____ a report to the secretary-general within six months.
2. He's come to the conclusion that over 90% of the variability of returns in institutional portfolios is _____ asset allocation.
3. Negotiators need to come up with, during the next week, solid proposals that can _____ the foundation stones an agreed outcome
4. You have questions about whether this high rate of growth is _____?
5. We cannot succeed in this _____ alone, but we can lead it, we can start it.

6. The Commission's _____ will be to inquire into the facts and circumstances of the assassination of former Prime Minister Bhutto.

II. **Read the following text and fill in the blanks with the words given in the box.**

| economics | introduction | renew | increasing | stemming |
| novelty | innovation | differently | relates | improvement |

Innovation comes from the Latin *innovationem*, noun of action from *innovare*. The Etymology Dictionary further explains *innovare* as dating back to 1540 and (1) _____ from the Latin *innovatus*, pp. of innovare "to (2) _____ or change," from in- "into" + novus "new". Innovation can therefore be seen as the process that renews or improves something that exists and not, as is commonly assumed, the (3) _____ of something better. Furthermore this makes clear (4) _____ is not an economic term by origin, but dates back to the Middle Ages at least. Possibly even earlier.

The central meaning of innovation thus (5) _____ to renewal or improvement. (6) _____ is just a consequence of improvement. For this (7) _____ to take place it is necessary for people to change the way they make decisions, they must choose to do things (8) _____, make choices outside of their norm.

Innovation is also an important topic in the study of (9) _____, it is also considered a major driver of the economy, especially when it leads to new product categories or (10) _____ productivity, the factors that lead to innovation are also considered to be critical to policy makers.

III. **Topic discussion.**
1. What are the four steps eBay takes with its employees? Can you illustrate them one by one?
2. What else can you find in eBay's good corporate culture besides the spirit of teamwork?

Supplementary Reading

The Fall of a Corporate Queen

AT&T, once one of the world's greatest companies, loses its independence.

From the very first words spoken over a telephone in 1876 by its inventor Alexander Graham Bell— "Mr. Watson, come here, I want to see you!"—AT&T always wanted to have its own way. And for much of its 128-year history, the American Telephone & Telegraph Company got it. First, as a brash start-up that won over 600 patent lawsuits in its first 18 years, then as a cut-throat competitor that pushed the limits of lawfulness to consolidate America's telecoms market and finally, until 1984, as a government-sanctioned monopoly.

But the modern era has been less generous, as the business behind AT&T's central activity of connecting long-distance calls crumbled. This week, SBC, one of the "baby bells" that was spun out of the company as part of a court-ordered break-up in 1984, acquired "Ma Bell", as AT&T is known, for around $16 billion, ending its reign as an independent firm. The new owner may yet adopt the famous brand as its corporate name. But the firm born in the 19th century, and which dominated the 20th, failed to survive long into the 21st.

The deal creates America's largest telecoms firm, with combined revenues of $70 billion and 210,000 employees (of which 10% are to be cut). AT&T had been for sale for a while, and had slashed debt and staff to pretty itself for suitors. SBC gets to sell to AT&T's millions of corporate customer's sophisticated data and voice services—around $20 billion of AT&T's revenues. The deal may prompt further consolidation (MCI is fingered as the next target by three other Bell companies, Qwest, Verizon and BellSouth), now that the period of internal rebuilding by telecoms firms after the bubble burst in 2000 is over.

For much of the past century AT&T was the envy of the corporate world—the largest firm on the planet both by revenue and market capitalization. No share was more widely held—the firm was so solid it was considered ideal for "widows and orphans". Its legendary research arm, Bell Laboratories, was responsible for some of the 20th century's greatest inventions, from the transistor to the laser, and fielded seven Nobel Prize winners. At the time of the break-up in 1984 AT&T boasted around 1 million employees. So what went wrong?

In short, the industry changed but AT&T failed to change with it. A century-old ethos of public service and reliability—thanks in part to its cosseted life as a protected monopoly with regulated rates—was ill-suited to competition in a world in which new technology cut the cost of calls and lowered rivals' barriers to entry. Despite owning the world's foremost corporate research lab, it missed moving into new technologies such as wireless and the Internet that would become the cornerstone of modern communications.

"It is a tragic fall and I lament the passing, because it was a huge disruptive success in its day", says Clayton Christensen of

Harvard Business School, author of the best-selling "Innovator's Dilemma". "The world is filled with companies that are marvellously innovative from a technical point of view, but completely unable to innovate on a business model." In the early 1980s, AT&T negotiated an antitrust settlement with the Department of Justice to separate its long-distance operation and create seven local telephone firms, spread across different regions. "AT&T will now be free", gushed *The Economist*, to put a computer on every desk connected by "broader-band links" and "pocket-mobile telephones in big cities". Yet at three critical junctures over the past two decades—involving wireless, computing and cable—the company misplayed its hand.

First, AT&T underestimated how important wireless communications would become. At the time of the break-up in 1984, AT&T relied on a report by McKinsey, a consultancy, which claimed there would be fewer than 1 million wireless phone users by 2000. In fact, there were 740 million. Cellular technology was then spotty—calls were often lost, the signal short and the power used by devices high—so AT&T declined to enter this small market. Until, that is, 1994, when it paid $11.5 billion for McCaw Cellular, which became AT&T Wireless and was sold last year for $41 billion.

The second stumble was in computing. After the break-up, AT&T expected to become a powerhouse in computers. Shedding the slow-moving local operators and retaining the Western Electric equipment business seemed a brilliant result from the antitrust process. AT&T even bought a computer maker, NCR, in 1991. But the fast-paced computing industry did not suit the stodgy former monopolist. And the equipment arm struggled because local operators declined to rely on a single supplier and gave half their business to other firms.

So, in 1995, AT&T voluntarily broke itself up still further, shedding Lucent, its re-named equipment maker, and NCR, at a huge financial loss. Now the downsized AT&T would focus on services.

This was the dawn of the commercial Internet, yet AT&T was nowhere. Two decades earlier it had dismissed the technology as unworkable, and later, as too small a market. It had even rejected numerous requests from American officials over three decades to operate the Internet backbone. Just as by inventing the transistor AT&T unleashed one of the central forces in technology that would eventually undermine the company, so it also missed the potential of the internet despite it running over its long-distance lines. In the 1970s, Bell Labs developed the UNIX computer operating system, which (evolved by others) still powers most of the world's large corporate computers. Alas, at that time AT&T was prevented by regulators from moving into computing, so UNIX was commercialized by others.

The third big mistake was to buy cable operators in the late 1990s. This was the right strategy at the wrong time and for too much money. At the height of the tech boom, AT&T's boss, Michael Armstrong, paid over $100 billion for two cable firms, TCI and Media One. AT&T realized it needed direct access to consumers, as it could no longer count on the regional bells, now moving into long-distance after the 1996 Telecom Act opened up competition in the sector. But the cable infrastructure required costly upgrades, and Ma Bell's domineering ways clashed with the cable firms' culture of co-operation.

Barely a year later, as the stock market turned on telecoms firms, AT&T faced a debt crisis. It had to abandon the firms it had just bought, and with them, the strategy of offering a basket of communications services including voice, TV and internet access—a strategy now regarded as the likeliest way to succeed.

"The main lesson is that it is very hard to change a culture that has evolved for a particular type of environment," says Andrew Odlyzko, a former Bell Labs researcher now at the University of Minnesota. AT&T grew up believing that communications comprised voice calls charged by the minute and the distance. But data subsumed voice, web traffic burst through the network via always-on broadband connections and distance is dead.

Is there a silver lining to this sorry tale? "It ought to be humbling to any empire-builder to see what was once the greatest corporation in America be acquired by one of its offspring", says Paul Starr, a communications historian at Princeton University. "But it's not necessarily a bad thing when the mighty lose sleep at night."

Tips

品牌管理：
1. 品牌管理的内涵

品牌是一种错综复杂的象征。它是品牌属性、名称、包装、价格、历史、信誉、广告方式的总称。品牌同时也是消费者留给其使用者的印象，以其自身的经验而有所界定。产品是工厂生产的东西，而品牌是消费者所购买的东西；产品可以被竞争者模仿，但品牌则是独一无二的；产品极易迅速过时落伍，但成功的品牌却能持久不坠，品牌的价值将长期影响企业。

对于很多中小型企业来说，品牌的内涵在一定程度上反映了企业文化，所以，对这种类型的企业来说，品牌不仅是对外（分销商、消费者）销售的利器，而且也是对内（员工、供应商）管理的道德力量。在营销中，品牌是唤起消费者重复消费的原始动力，是消费市场上的灵魂。没有品牌，企业就没有灵魂；没有品牌，企业就会失去生命力。

2. 怎样进行成功的品牌管理？

品牌管理是个复杂的、科学的过程，不可以省略任何一个环节。下面是成功的品牌管理应该遵守的四个步骤。

第一步：勾画出品牌的"精髓"，即描绘品牌的理性因素。

首先，把品牌现有的可以用事实和数字勾画的看得见摸得着的人力、物力、财力找出来，其次，根据目标再描绘出需要增加哪些人力、物力和财力才可以使品牌的精髓部分变得更充实。这里包括消费群体的信息、员工的构成、投资人和战略伙伴的关系、企业的结构、市场的状况、竞争格局等。

第二步：掌握品牌的"核心"，即描绘品牌的感性因素。

由于品牌和人一样除了有躯体和四肢外还有思想和感觉，所以在了解现有品牌的核心时必须了解它的文化渊源、社会责任、消费者的心理因素和情绪因素并将感情因素考虑在内。根据要实现的目标，重新定位品牌的核心并将需要增加的感性因素一一列出来。

第三步：寻找品牌的灵魂，即找到品牌与众不同的求异战略。

通过第一步和第二步对品牌理性和感性因素的了解和评估，升华品牌的灵魂及独一无二的定位和宣传信息。人们喜欢去麦当劳用餐，是因为它带给儿童和成年人一份安宁和快乐的感受。人们喜欢去 Disney 乐园游玩，是因为人们可以在那里找到童年的梦想和乐趣。所以品牌不是产品和服务本身，而是它留给人们的想象和感觉。品牌的灵魂就代表了这样的感觉和感受。

第四步：品牌的培育、保护及长期爱护。

品牌形成容易但维持是一个很艰难的过程。没有很好的品牌关怀战略，品牌是无法成长的。很多品牌只靠花掉大量的资金做广告来增加客户资源，但由于不知道品牌管理的科学过程，在有了品牌知名度后，不再关注客户需求的变化，不能提供承诺的一流服务，失望的客户只能无奈地选择新的品牌，致使花掉大把的钱得到的品牌效应昙花一现。所以，品牌管理的重点是品牌的维护。

3. 品牌管理的四个重点要素
建立卓越的信誉；争取广泛的支持；建立亲密的关系；增加亲身体验的机会。

4. 品牌管理的价值法则
最优化的管理；最优化的产品；亲密的客户关系。

Unit 11

Business Ethics and Corprate Social Responsibility

Text A　The Corporate Responsibility Commitment

> 导读：企业社会责任是指企业在创造利润、对股东承担法律责任的同时，还要承担对员工、消费者、社区和环境的责任。其要求企业必须超越把利润作为唯一目标的传统理念，强调在生产过程中对人的价值的关注，强调对消费者、对环境、对社会的贡献。企业社会责任作为一种新的企业经营策略已被越来越多的公司和机构采用，因为良好的企业社会责任会给公司带来长远而巨大的效益是一个毋庸置疑的事实。

Corporate Responsibility and Corporate Social Responsibility sit among those sets of initials—like B2B, CRM, SME—that have simply become similated into everyday business speak. CR is a broader term for CSR. To understand what these initials literally stand for is the easy part but, as a casual trawl of the Web will reveal, to define what corporate responsibility or the older term corporate social responsibility means has not proved so simple.

There are myriad definitions of corporate social responsibility, with analysts seemingly divided on whether it is the "Corporate", the "Social" or the "Responsibility" that demands the most focus. Along with this confusion of meaning comes a host of bold claims that seemingly position corporate social responsibility as the Holy Grail. Little wonder that businesses of every size are both irresistibly attracted to corporate social responsibility but also somewhat daunted by the prospect of meeting such grand expectations.

It is up to companies then to define for themselves what those expectations should be. As a company, Pitney Bowes has decided to use the term corporate responsibility, extending the concept to caring for the environment and seeing to the proper disposal and recycling of equipment and consumables. It means taking on responsibilities beyond the "social" and committing to having a positive impact on the physical state of the community as well.

It is important to remember that there are no hard and fast rules for corporate responsibility programs although there are general guidelines emerging such as those from the Global Reporting Initiative, an independent institution that provides a framework for tracking social and environmental activities. Still, there is no precise definition of what a corporate responsibility program should encompass, but there are definite pitfalls to avoid.

Commitment and Budget

Certainly, there is little point in a corporate responsibility program for the sake of it. Arguably, businesses that take up a corporate responsibility initiative in a bid to appear forward-thinking and progressive, only to then withdraw once the spotlight moves to the next business trend, will do themselves more harm than good. Any corporate responsibility policy must represent a long-term commitment—which takes planning, staff commitment and budget.

Equally, businesses should avoid over-committing and making promises that simply aren't realistic or affordable. Businesses are not charities and there should be no shame in being overt about the commercial advantages that a strong corporate responsibility program can deliver.

When looking at our own program, a major consideration was that much of the activity should relate back to our core business. We run an annual auction event called "Pushing the Envelope" to raise funds for the National Literacy Trust (NLT). We got involved with the NLT five years ago because, as a company, Pitney Bowes is all about improving communications for our customers. The National Literacy Trust (NLT) is driving to improve standards of literacy across all age groups-and improved literacy obviously means improved communication.

The "Pushing the Envelope" event relates back to our core business activity because we ask celebrities and artists to design envelopes. The fact that these designs are on envelopes makes the event stand out, but also references our core strength of mail and messaging technology.

On the environmental side, Pitney Bowes takes back equipment and either disposes of it responsibly-recycling parts and recovering precious metals-or refurbishes it to sell in other markets. The company is committed to protecting the environment and is an accredited ISO 14001 company.

A Differentiator

There is clear evidence that customers are beginning to expect the businesses they deal with to be corporate responsibility advocates—taking on social responsibilities and meeting green standards. In the consumer market, businesses are dedicating significant budget to declaring their corporate responsibility colors.

In the business to business arena, corporate responsibility is by no means yet a critical influencer. But, in a competitive market, corporate responsibility can represent a differentiator from competitors and an area of common ground with clients in initial new business discussions.

Equally, corporate responsibility can be important for improving a company's standing in its own community—which in turn can aid the recruitment process. Similarly, existing employees like to feel part of a company that is seen to be responsible and "giving back" to the wider community.

Of course, as with any new business strategy, corporate responsibility has its detractors. Critics argue that corporate responsibility distracts from the fundamental economic role of businesses while others argue that it is nothing more than superficial window-dressing.

Certainly, our own involvement with the National Literacy Trust has been well received by both staff and customers. But more than this—and a point that's often overlooked—it's been enormous fun! Pitney Bowes has been able to align its brand to such stellar names as Damien Hirst, Sir Ian McKellan, Kate Winslet and hundreds of others, whilst raising much valued funds for an extremely deserving cause.

The message is—don't simply adopt corporate responsibility for the sake of it.

Think long-term, find relationships that make sense for your brand and be creative. Big businesses can often be accused of a myopic, navel-gazing approach but sensible corporate responsibility partnerships suggest a company that is more aware of its wider role.

Corporate responsibility champions argue that there is a strong business case in that corporations benefit in multiple ways by operating with a perspective broader and longer than their own immediate, short-term profits. Whatever one's personal opinion there is little doubt that corporate responsibility is no flash-in-the-pan and that, increasingly, consumers and organizations are looking to do business with companies that display this broader perspective.

Notes:

1. **Customer Relationship Management（客户关系管理，缩写 CRM）:** is a broadly recognized, widely-implemented strategy for managing a company's interactions with customers, clients and sales prospects. It involves using technology to organize, automate, and synchronize business processes—principally sales activities, but also those for marketing, customer service, and technical support. The overall goals are to find, attract, and win new clients, nurture and retain those the company already has, entice former clients back into the fold, and reduce the costs of marketing and client service.

2. **SME（中小型企业）:** Small and Medium Enterprises (also SMEs, small and medium businesses, SMBs, and variations thereof) are companies whose headcount or turnover falls below certain limits. The abbreviation SME occurs commonly in the European Union and in international organizations, such as the World Bank, the United Nations and the WTO. The term small and medium businesses or SMBs is predominantly used in the USA.

3. **Holy Grail（圣杯）:** The Holy Grail is a sacred object figuring in literature and certain Christian traditions, most often identified with the dish, plate, or cup used by Jesus at the Last Supper and said to possess miraculous powers.

4. **the National Literacy Trust（英国国家文教信托）:** The National Literacy Trust (NLT) is an independent charity based in London, England, that transforms lives through literacy.

Founded in 1993, the NLT brings together partners in education and the community in innovative ways, working towards a society in which everyone has the reading, writing, speaking and listening skills they need to fulfill their potential.

5. ISO 14001（国际环境管理体系标准）: It is part of a family of 16 international ISO 14,000 standards designed to assist companies in reducing their negative impact on the environment. The standard is not an environmental management system as such and therefore does not dictate absolute environmental performance requirements, but serves instead as a framework to assist organizations in developing there own environmental management system.

Words & Expressions：

1. assimilate [ə'simileit] vt. 吸收；使同化；把……比作；使相似
   vi. 吸收；同化
2. myriad ['miriəd] adj. 无数的；种种的
   n. 无数，极大数量；无数的人或物
3. daunt [dɔ:nt] vt. 使气馁，使畏缩；威吓
4. disposal [dis'pəuzəl] n. 处理；支配；清理；安排
5. consumable [kən'sju:məbl] n. 消费品；消耗品
   adj. 可消耗的；可消费的
6. pitfall ['pitfɔ:l] n. 缺陷；陷阱，圈套；诱惑
7. encompass [in'kʌmpəs] vt. 包含；包围，环绕；完成
8. in a bid to　为了……
9. refurbish [ri:'fə:biʃ] vt. 刷新；再磨光
10. arena [ə'ri:nə] n. 舞台；竞技场
11. overt ['əuvə:t, əu'və:t] adj. 明显的；公然的；[律] 蓄意的
12. detractor [di'træktə] n. 贬低者；诽谤者

13. accredited [əˈkreditid] adj. 公认的；可信任的
14. recruitment [riˈkruːtmənt] n. 补充；征募新兵；招聘，聘任，人员招募
15. myopic [maiˈɔpik] adj. [眼科] 近视的；目光短浅的
16. align [əˈlain] vt. 使结盟；使成一行；匹配
    vi. 排列；排成一行
17. stellar [ˈstelə] adj. 星（状的）；和电影明星有关的；主要的；一流的；极好的
18. navel-gazing: 纸上谈兵
19. flash-in-the-pan: 昙花一现的人或物
20. window-dressing: [ˈwindəuˌdresiŋ] n. 装门面措施；弄虚作假
    vt. 布置橱窗；装饰门面

Exercises:

Ⅰ. Fill in the blanks with the suitable words given in the box. Change the form when necessary.

| myopic | encompass | overt | assimilate |
| refurbish | arena | daunt | accredited |

1. The sports _____, now called Verizon Center, brought new life to this area of the city.
2. Why is it so difficult for us to understand, accept, _____ and live according to the fact that we can make a difference?
3. Leaders of the world's most populous nation have issued orders to build or _____ 1,000 museums by 2010.
4. Once we master it, no material difficulties can _____ us.
5. She criticized any _____ display of emotion and attempts at open rebellion against the Ruling Power.
6. When some people are choosing a spouse, afraid also sweetheart is _____, whether to meet complicity child.

7. Here's how you become an _____ investor: you have $1 million dollars in investable—that's not including your house, it's in investable assets.

8. Our relations have been transformed, and today they _____ cooperation in all areas of human activity.

Ⅱ. Read the following text and fill in the blanks with the words given in the box.

| governmental | accelerated | codes | relevant | corporate |
| interaction | laws | arise | normative | ethical |

Business ethics (also known as (1) _____ ethics) is a form of applied ethics or professional ethics that examines (2) _____ principles and moral or ethical problems that (3) _____ in a business environment. It applies to all aspects of business conduct and is (4) _____ to the conduct of individuals and entire organizations. Business ethics has both (5) _____ and descriptive dimensions. As a corporate practice and a career specialization, the field is primarily normative. Academics attempting to understand business behavior employ descriptive methods. The range and quantity of business ethical issues reflects the (6) _____ of profit-maximizing behavior with non-economic concerns. Interest in business ethics (7) _____ dramatically during the 1980s and 1990s, both within major corporations and within academia. For example, today most major corporations promote their commitment to non-economic values under headings such as ethics (8) _____ and social responsibility charters. Governments use (9) _____ and regulations to point business behavior in what they perceive to be beneficial directions. Ethics implicitly regulates areas and details of behavior that lie beyond (10) _____ control.

Ⅲ. Decide whether the following statements are true (T) or false (F) according to the passage.

1. The fact that corporate social responsibility both attracts and daunts businesses of every size is quite incredible. ( )

2. With general guidelines emerging from the Global Reporting Initiative, companies are required to follow the strict rules for corporate responsibility programs. ( )

3. A long-term commitment should be taken into consideration when the corporate responsibility policy is being formulated. (   )
4. Unlike charities, businesses are reluctant to expose the commercial advantages that could be delivered by a strong corporate responsibility program. (   )
5. Pitney Bowes's successful involvement with the National Literacy Trust also serves as a long-term beneficial strategy for the company. (   )

Text B Controversial Chemical Poses Challenge for Colgate-Palmolive

> **导读**：商业伦理是一门关于商业与伦理学的交叉学科。商业伦理研究的是商业活动中人与人的伦理关系及其规律，研究使商业和商业主体既充满生机又有利于人类全面和谐发展的合理的商业伦理秩序。商业伦理从分析商业的本质、商务活动的前期行为入手，为人们提供了判断商务活动是否符合道德规范的商业道德行为准则。

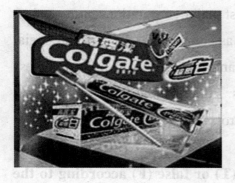

A feisty debate over the safety of a widely used chemical has put Colgate-Palmolive at the center of a case study in product disclosure and corporate responsibility—one that may ultimately help outline how companies wading through a murky regulatory review and unsettled science should attend to their stakeholders and customers.

The current squeeze on Colgate stems from a U. S. Food and Drug Administration decision this year to train its microscopes more closely on triclosan, a chemical with antibacterial properties that in recent decades has been added to scores of products, but now is under new scrutiny because of studies that suggest it may harm both human health and the environment. And while the FDA conducts its review—and critics of triclosan mount their arguments to curtail its use by consumers—Colgate and other product manufacturers have to decide what they can and should say to the marketplace, not to mention when and how to convey it.

The hurdle the company faces is clear: a core ingredient of its top-selling Colgate Total toothpaste is suddenly the heart of a public health tempest, but regulators have neither banned the chemical nor deemed it unsafe. There is no well-tested playbook for the scenario, says David Nash, partner at McMahon DeGulis, an environmental law firm based in Cleveland.

"The dilemma becomes, what kind of legal, moral, or socially responsible duty do they have to stakeholders to go beyond where the regulatory agency has already gone?" he asks. "In this fast-moving field, I would be hard-pressed to say there is a consensus on best practices."

It complicates matters for Colgate that few products have gotten more mileage out of triclosan than Colgate Total, which won special FDA approval in 1997 for its use of the chemical in a patented formula to prevent gingivitis, a common form of gum disease. In short order, Colgate Total vaulted above competitors to become the top-selling product, and today it remains a big contributor to Colgate's worldwide 44.4% share of the global toothpaste market and its 35.6% slice of the U. S. market, according to company filings this year. At the beginning of last year, Colgate announced that among its toothpaste varieties, the Colgate Total brand by itself had 16% of the overall market in North America.

Another thorny issue for Colgate is that the FDA is heightening attention on triclosan (PDF) at the same time it serves as the first line of defense against critics. That's because on the one hand, the FDA is teaming up with other federal regulators, particularly the Environmental Protection Agency (PDF), to sponsor new research on triclosan's safety. But on the other, the FDA has issued a statement that "triclosan is not currently known to be hazardous to humans" and that the agency "does not have sufficient safety evidence to recommend changing consumer use of products that contain triclosan at this time" —and won't have its first answers until spring 2011.

That leaves product makers with decisions that perhaps they would not have faced even 10 years ago, when corporate social responsibility factored far less in the strategic thinking at most companies. Should a company proactively inform its customers that a key ingredient of its product is facing questions? Should it amend its marketing? Should it play an active role in the scientific debate? Should it publicly defend its turf? Should it simply do nothing and wait?

Colgate's response to date largely has been to point those who specifically ask about triclosan to the FDA's prior approval of Colgate Total. A company spokeswoman points to a statement on the FDA website (PDF) that says, "In 1997, FDA reviewed extensive effectiveness data on triclosan in Colgate Total toothpaste. The evidence showed that triclosan in this product was effective in preventing gingivitis." Colgate's own statement adds that since the approval, "Colgate has routinely provided FDA with updated information, consistent with the agency's guidelines, and is confident that further study will continue to add to the substantial body of research that affirms the safety of triclosan in Colgate Total."

It's a detached defense, sticking to discussion of its product and not engaging in the greater triclosan debate. What time will tell is whether Colgate is telling consumers enough to position itself best for when the FDA makes a final determination on triclosan, says Barbara Burton of The Burton Company in La Jolla, Calif., a corporate responsibility consultant.

"You have to determine what to disclose," she adds. "When you're not disclosing what you should, you assume risk."

Nash says the corporate social responsibility issues Colgate faces—and their impact on how the company communicates with consumers—are bound to repeat themselves in other industries and settings. He points to prominent cases from just the past year, citing Toyota's struggle with scrutiny on accidents involving its vehicles that were attributed by some to faulty equipment; the firestorm that Goldman Sachs faced when securities regulators essentially accused it of cheating its customers; and BP's very public missteps in the wake of its giant Gulf of Mexico oil spill. And Nash says the rules of engagement for these episodes are in constant flux.

"Science changes," he adds. "Medicine changes. So does perception. So does politics. So does tolerance for risk."

Widespread Use and Unknown Impact

Triclosan is hardly just Colgate's concern, but its wide use actually makes matters trickier for the company. The chemical-first developed in the 1960s by Ciba—appears in products as varied as clothing, kitchenware, furniture, toys, and even food, says Douglas Throckmorton, deputy director for regulatory programs at the FDA's Center for Drug Evaluation and Research. "Every time I've asked for a list of products using triclosan, they say, 'Beware—we're sure we're missing some,'" he says.

One of the most prominent uses, however, is in antibacterial soaps, hand sanitizers, and body washes, and that's where the current debate is centered. Throckmorton says that since 1994, the FDA has been working on its "monograph" of definitive rules governing the use of ingredients such as triclosan in these products, and that until the work finishes, companies can use these kinds of substances. The slow progress is what inspired critics of the process to step up their arguments this year that the monograph's delay was allowing products to continue using triclosan despite new research studies indicating it is unsafe.

It's notable that Colgate isn't at the nucleus of the debate. Throckmorton says Colgate's use of triclosan doesn't fall under the proposed monograph, or even under a separate pending monograph for toothpastes, because its 1997 "new drug application" approval from the FDA was built on extensive and specific studies showing Colgate Total's "safety and efficacy" in preventing gingivitis. That means even if the agency were to ban triclosan from hand soaps, Colgate could still use it in Colgate Total.

For now, the scientific dispute has several fronts. Throckmorton says the FDA's announcement in April that it was coordinating with the EPA and other agencies to further study triclosan stems from research studies in recent years analyzing the chemical's potential impact on animal reproductive systems; its possible carcinogenic effects on skin; its widespread appearance in environmental and population samples; and its role in antimicrobial resistance. One of the biggest concerns is its potential as an "endocrine disruptor," which means that it can alter hormone behavior.

Most recent studies have traced triclosan's impact on animals, although its pervasiveness in humans is clear. The federal Centers for Disease Control and Prevention reported several years ago that it found triclosan in the urine of three-quarters of participants in a 2,500-person health survey.

Some public health advocacy groups say growing evidence points to triclosan's negative health effects, and have urged the FDA to act swiftly. The Natural Resources Defense Council filed a lawsuit against the FDA in July 2010 to force the agency to finish its soaps monograph. And the FDA's April announcement to step up its review appears to have been pushed by inquiries from Rep. Edward Markey of Massachusetts, who chairs a House panel on energy and the environment and has asked the agency to restrict triclosan use.

Arguing the opposite case have been triclosan's defenders, particularly chemical companies that make the substance for commercial use as well as industry groups such as the American Cleaning Institute, which dismisses the critics as fear-mongerers and contends that products with the substance have been used safely for decades in homes, hospitals, and offices.

Colgate has been on the periphery of the debate because of its special approval status. But any negative finding against triclosan would undoubtedly impact the company. And both NRDC and Markey have called on the FDA to revisit its approval of triclosan in Colgate Total.

"We didn't have data on the endocrine disruptor effect when it was approved," says Sarah Janssen, senior scientist for NRDC. "We have asked the FDA to review those applications and determine whether it really does meet that bar of being safe."

Exposure and Disclosure

As the triclosan debate swirls, Colgate has planted itself behind the FDA's 1997 blessing of Colgate Total as well as similar endorsements, such as the product's clearance for use in 173 countries and seals of approval from dental associations. The spokeswoman declines to go beyond the company's basic statement, saying, "We are unavailable to further discuss." It also is not openly combating the critics raising general questions about the chemical.

McMahon DeGulis partner Nash says Colgate is "absolutely entitled" to stand on its FDA approval as a valid response to questions.

But that doesn't dismiss the question of whether Colgate ought to tell customers about the broader argument over triclosan's safety. Burton, the consultant, says the tide is turning toward greater disclosure, particularly with initiatives such as the United Nations Global Compact and the development of the International Organization for Standardization's 26000 standard on social responsibility, which calls for broad transparency with stakeholders on matters related to product safety.

"You don't want to take the chance of not disclosing information about potential safety concerns," she says.

She adds that while wide disclosure in a case like Colgate's could have a negative short-term impact on market share, it also could generate long-term customer good will.

However, in instances as messy as the triclosan safety debate, there is also risk of disclosing data that simply breeds confusion, says Ken Strassner of Strassner Consulting in Sandy Springs, Ga. "I do not believe that you have to automatically disclose everything," he adds. "There is a fair amount of consumer research that shows people don't understand the science."

There is also the concern of disclosing information that could wrongly inflame fear among customers. "We talk to our clients about being transparent, but doing it in a smart, responsible way," Nash says.

Indeed, a company faces risk management questions if inappropriate disclosure exposes "the company to frivolous legal action or risk to its share price or to the investing community," he adds.

In order to decide what to disclose, Strassner says a company must fully understand the "best available science."

That's also critical for risk management, because a company needs to vet the "credibility and validity of the data," as well as the scientists conducting the studies, to ensure "advocacy science" is not driving decisions, Nash says.

Strassner also says a company in Colgate's situation should stay engaged in the overall review, offering its technical expertise and input on findings. "I would participate in these processes in an open, straightforward, technical way," he adds. "I'm not suggesting you run to the head of FDA and say 'Kill the investigation.'"

If Colgate's case underscores how balancing socially responsible conduct with company interests is more than ever a tightrope walk, it also should remind corporate leaders that such challenges are sure to multiply.

"We're in a very complex society with very complex technology," Nash says. "Frankly, this kind of stuff is going to come up again, and I think it's going to come more frequently."

Notes:

1. Colgate-Palmolive Company（高露洁棕榄有限公司）: is an American diversified multinational corporation focused on the production, distribution and provision of household, health care and personal products, such as soaps, detergents, and oral hygiene products (including toothpaste and toothbrushes). Under its "Hill's" brand, it is also a manufacturer of veterinary products. The company's corporate offices are on Park Avenue in Midtown Manhattan, New York City.

2. Toyota Motor Corporation（丰田汽车公司）: (Japanese: *Toyota Jidōsha Kabushiki-gaisha*) is commonly known simply as Toyota and abbreviated as TMC, is a multinational corporation headquartered in Japan.

3. FDA（U. S. Food and Drug Administration（美国食品和药物管理局）: is an agency of the United States Department of Health and Human Services, one of the United States federal executive departments. The FDA is responsible for protecting and promoting public health through the regulation and supervision of food safety, tobacco products, dietary supplements, prescription and over-the-counter pharmaceutical drugs (medications), vaccines, biopharmaceuticals, blood transfusions, medical devices, electromagnetic radiation emitting devices (ERED), veterinary products, and cosmetics.

4. Goldman Sachs（高盛集团）: is a global investment banking and securities firm that engages in investment banking, securities, investment management, and other financial services primarily with institutional clients. Goldman Sachs was founded in 1869 and is headquartered at 200 West Street in the Lower Manhattan area of New York City, with additional offices in major international financial centers.

Words & Expressions:

1. feisty ['faisti] adj. 活跃的；好争吵的；烦躁不安的
2. disclosure [dis'kləuʒə] n. 披露；揭发；被揭发出来的事情
3. murky ['məːki] adj. 黑暗的；朦胧的；阴郁的
4. stakeholder ['steik,həuldə] n. 利益相关者；赌金保管者
5. squeeze [skwiːz] vt. 挤；紧握；勒索
   vi. 压榨
   n. 压榨；紧握；拥挤；佣金
6. curtail [kəː'teil] vt. 缩减；剪短；剥夺……特权等
7. scenario [si'nɑːriəu] n. 方案；情节；剧本
8. consensus [kən'sensəs] n. 一致；舆论；合意
9. mileage ['mailidʒ] n. 英里数
10. formula ['fɔːmjulə] n. 公式，准则；配方；婴儿食品
11. gingivitis [,dʒindʒi'vaitis] n. 齿龈炎
12. thorny ['θɔːni] adj. 多刺的；痛苦的；令人苦恼的
13. sponsor ['spɔnsə] n. 赞助者；主办者；保证人
    vt. 赞助；发起
14. hazardous ['hæzədəs] adj. 有危险的；冒险的；碰运气的
15. proactively [,prəu'æktivli] adv. 前摄地
16. detached [di'tætʃt] adj. 分离的，分开的；超然的
17. prominent ['prɔminənt] adj. 突出的，显著的；杰出的；卓越的
18. scrutiny ['skruːtini] n. 详细审查；监视；细看；选票复查
19. episode ['episəud] n. 插曲；一段情节；插话；有趣的事件
20. carcinogenic [,kɑːsinəu'dʒenik] adj. 致癌的；致癌物的

Exercises:

Ⅰ. Fill in the blanks with the suitable words given in the box. Change the form when necessary.

scrutiny	episode	application	available	squeeze
inform	management	detached	participate	prominent

1. He _____ the tube hard and the last bit of toothpaste came out.
2. A judge must be _____ when weighing evidence.
3. It is important that China play an increasingly _____ role on climate change.
4. The merits of infrastructure investment are the latest to come under _____.
5. If you choose to delete the _____ and file, they will be permanently lost.
6. This workflow now contains the business logic for an _____ for processing credit cards.
7. While walking the guest to the elevator, _____ the guest his room number and on what floor he would be in.
8. Good at planning, good at time _____.
9. We can recommend any of our friends to _____ in your project!
10. The basic idea of our tool is that we can collect many different data under different _____ bandwidth.

Ⅱ. Translate the following sentences into Chinese.

1. The current squeeze on Colgate stems from a U. S. Food and Drug Administration decision this year to train its microscopes more closely on triclosan, a chemical with antibacterial properties that in recent decades has been added to scores of products, but now is under new scrutiny because of studies that suggest it may harm both human health and the environment.

2. Most recent studies have traced triclosan's impact on animals, although its pervasiveness in humans is clear.

3. Although many people tend to live under the illusion that traditional technology and methods are still playing extremely important role in people's life, an increasing evidences show that it is less useful than many people think.
4. The reason for such rapid growth in China-U. S. trade is, in the final analysis, the high degree to which the economies complement each other. This neat fit, to a large extent, stems from their differences in economic resources, economic structures and consumption levels.
5. Information age organizations can manage the complexity of the large hierarchical structure without losing the speed of the entrepreneurial start-ups.

III. Exploring questions.

Please find more information about "circular economy" from TV, newspapers and the Internet.

Supplementary Reading

Toyota Recall: Five Critical Lessons

Toyota's announcement of a technical fix for its sticky gas pedals—which can lead to sudden acceleration problems—is not likely to bring a quick end to the company's current recall nightmare.

Having already halted sales and production of eight of its top-selling cars in the U. S.—and recalled more than 9 million cars worldwide, in two separate recalls—Toyota faces the prospect of billions of dollars in charges and operating losses. The Toyota brand, once almost synonymous with top quality, has taken a heavy hit.

While all the facts are not yet in, it's clear that Toyota's crisis didn't emerge full-blown overnight. Fixing the problem and ensuring that something like it doesn't happen again will require an all-out effort, from assembly line to the boardroom. Even then, there are no guarantees. Maintaining a good corporate reputation in the 21st century is tricky business indeed.

Toyota's case offers a number of valuable lessons for other business people and companies to consider. Here, for starters, are five:

Aggressive growth can create unmanageable risk. Toyota's desire to supplant General Motors as the world's number—one car—maker pushed it to the outer limits of quality control.

"The evidence that Toyota was expanding too much and too quickly started surfacing a couple of years ago. Not on the company's bottom line, but on its car-quality ratings," writes Paul Ingrassia, a Pulitzer Prize-winning former Detroit bureau chief for *The Wall Street Journal*.

Ingrassia, who has just authored a new book on the auto industry, notes that in 2005 Toyota recalled more cars and trucks than it sold; by 2007, Consumer Reports magazine stopped automatically recommending all Toyota models because of quality declines on three models.

One wonders if, when accepting management's plan for aggressive growth, Toyota's board of directors exercised appropriate diligence to ensure that growth could be achieved without betting the entire franchise. Were quality control and safety part of the discussion? Maybe gaining market share wasn't worth the trade-off. Quick tip to directors of other high-growth-oriented companies: read up on Merrill Lynch's experience with dominating the sub-prime mortgage market.

Get the facts quickly and manage your risks aggressively. One of the more troubling aspects of Toyota's recalls (there have been two) has been the company's differing accounts of the source of the problem. The current recall, covering 4.1 million cars, involves potentially sticky gas pedals. Late in 2009, Toyota also recalled 5.4 million cars whose gas pedals could get stuck on floor mats. Plus, Toyota says there are some cars affected by both problems. (For an interesting technical analysis of some of the issues involved, go here.)

Uncertainty is not an asset, especially when lives could be at stake. A Los Angeles Times investigation, for example, casts doubt on Toyota's explanation, quoting one auto safety consulting group as saying, "We know this recall is a red herring." (Read Toyota's position here.)

And the questioning is just beginning. A U. S. Congressional committee headed by Rep. Henry Waxman has already requested copies of E-mails and other documents from both Toyota and the National Highway Traffic Safety Administration, which regulates Toyota with regard to the recalls. Congressional hearings are scheduled for Feb. 25.

In cases such as this, investigators almost always start with two time-worn questions. *What did you know? And when did you know it?* Answers to those questions provide the groundwork for analysis of a company's response and handling of a problem. Were employees encouraged to flag safety issues to senior management? Were sufficient resources devoted to investigating the problems? When did the board become aware of the situation and what did it do about it?

Companies generally can't predict when crises might occur. However, good internal risk assessment programs can help identify those areas of the business where management should be on the alert. Robust risk management programs help a company address problems as they pop up on the internal corporate radar screen-and before they explode in public.

Your supply chain is only as strong as your weakest link. The reality is that auto companies make hardly any of their parts. They *assemble* cars from parts made by others. In this case, the offending gas pedal assembly was made for Toyota by a company called CTS of Elkhardt, Indiana.

It's far from certain how much blame the parts supplier deserves. In fact, CTS says Toyota's acceleration problems date back to 1999, years before CTS began supplying parts to Toyota. (And the replacement gas pedal parts Toyota has announced as a fix for the problem will be made by CTS, suggesting a degree of confidence in the supplier.)

Nonetheless, "if you are outsourcing for your entire vehicle line, and the outsourced component is defective, the recall and the embarrassment are much greater," iconic car company critic Ralph Nader told Toronto's *Globe and Mail* last week. "The overall message is that quality control means daily vigilance," Nader said. "You can't coast on your reputation because it can fail very quickly."

Supply chain monitoring is a critical factor for companies that rely on third-party suppliers. That's increasingly true for a broad variety of industries, not just automobiles, as business grows ever more global. Smart companies will know their suppliers and their respective strengths and weaknesses.

Accept Responsibility. This is one area where Toyota seems to be doing a good job, albeit maybe a year or more too late.

Toyota's National Ad on Recall—January 31, 2010

Two decades ago, when Audi encountered a safety issue similar to Toyota's, Audi took the position that "it was the driver's fault," David Cole, Director of the Center for Automotive Research, told Design News. Coles says that reaction ultimately hurt Audi's reputation.

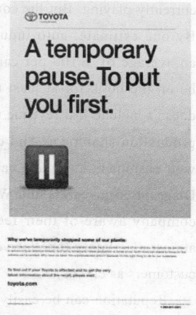

Toyota seems to be avoiding the appearance of passing the buck. When pressed by the *New York Times* about problems that might have been caused by supplier CTS, for example, Toyota spokesman Mike Michels said: "I don't want to get into any kind of a disagreement with CTS. Our position on suppliers has always been that Toyota is responsible for the cars."

Accountability matters enormously. Johnson & Johnson's 1982 recall of its painkiller Tylenol, following the deaths of seven people in the Chicago area, has earned it a permanent place in the annals of crisis management. But that recall stemmed from the deadly act of an outsider (who has never been caught), not any problem with the product itself, as is the case with Toyota.

Take the Long View. The three leading factors burnishing corporate reputation these days are "quality products and services, a company I can trust and transparency of business practices," writes public relations executive Richard Edelman, who last week released his corporate "Trust Barometer" survey for 2010.

That's unfortunate news for Toyota, given the hand that it's currently playing. But the company doesn't have much choice. By one estimate, auto industry recalls conservatively cost an average of ＄100 per car—suggesting that Toyota might be on the hook for at least a one billion dollar charge. That doesn't include lost revenue to Toyota and its dealers from the production shutdown. And competitors are already trying to woo customers away and capitalize on Toyota's misfortune. Disgruntled investors and Wall Street analysts will make the company aware of their feelings; class action lawsuits are almost a certainty (one lawyer is already searching for Toyota customers as clients).

Reputation can be easily lost—and Toyota's reputation is indeed threatened—but it's highly unlikely the company will collapse completely. And that may be one of the biggest lessons for other companies as they study how Toyota emerges from this recall crisis. The reality is that Toyota is positioned for recovery about as well as it could be—owing, in large measure, to the reputation for quality products and corporate responsibility it has developed over the last two decades. That reputation is a valuable asset, and one that Toyota will undoubtedly be citing and calling upon, in the weeks and months ahead.

Tips

日本九大汽车公司：
1. 丰田汽车公司（TOYOTA）

丰田汽车公司是日本最大的汽车公司，由丰田喜一郎创立于1933年，总部设在日本爱知县丰田市和东京都文京区。世界五百强第8位。丰田公司知名品牌极多，丰田、皇冠、光冠、花冠曾名噪一时，而近年新推出的克雷西达、凌志豪华车也享誉世界车坛。现在丰田集团还控股了日野汽车公司和大发汽车公司。

2. 日产汽车公司（NISSAN）

日本汽车公司是日本的第二大汽车公司，也是世界十大汽车公司之一。创立于1933年，1934年开始使用现名"日产汽车公司"。总部现设在日本东京市，雇员总数超过15万人。年产汽车320万辆。日产汽车公司的汽车品牌众多，货车类品牌有巴宁、途乐、皮卡和佳碧等，豪华型轿车有公爵、蓝鸟、千里马、无限、光荣、桂冠和总统等，普通型轿车则有阳光、自由别墅、地平线和兰利等，此外还有无限45跑车等。

3. 三菱汽车公司（MITSUBISHI）

三菱汽车公司是日本三菱集团成员之一，1970年从三菱重工业公司脱离，正式成立三菱汽车工业有限公司。由三菱重工业公司和美国克莱斯勒公司共同出资组建，公司总部设在东京港区，全球排名第十五大汽车制造者。主要产品有微型轿车和载货汽车、小型轿车和载货车、中重型载货车、厢式车、客车、运动车、发动机和其他零部件等。

4. 马自达汽车公司（MAZDA）

马自达汽车公司由松田创立于1920年，原名东洋软木工业公司，1984年公司以创始人松田的姓氏命名，翻译时则采用"松田"的音译"马自达"。公司总部设在日本广岛县安芸君府中町，公司排名位居世界20家最大汽车公司之列，以生产转子发动机汽车而闻名。这种发动机采用微机控制发动机负载状态，自动调整怠速装置和废气再循环装置，使发动机工作平稳，从而降低油耗，减少废气的排出。

5. 本田汽车公司（HONDA）

本田汽车公司由本田宗一郎创立于1948年，早年以生产摩托车为主，现仍为世界最大的摩托车生产厂商。1960年后本田走向汽车发展之路，1976年推出第一代"雅阁"（Accord），现已推出第6代，该车在1989年曾登上美国同级轿车销量冠军。本田的其他轿车品牌还有阿科达、市民、序曲、都市等。

6. 铃木汽车公司（SUZUKI）

铃木的前身是一间纺织机械制造厂，20世纪50年代初转产摩托车和汽车，并于1954年正式命名为铃木汽车公司，总部设在日本静冈县，以生产微型汽车为主。铃木品牌既有摩托车也有汽车，虽然铃木汽车的知名度比摩托车逊色，但在世界车坛上也居相当高的位置。铃木摩托车早在二十世纪八十年代已经进入中国内地销售。铃木主要汽车品牌有吉姆尼、武士、奥拓等，其中奥拓汽车已引入中国生产。

7. 五十铃汽车（ISUZU）

五十铃公司的前身是东京石川岛造船所，1920年起与英国Wolseley公司合作生产轿车，1949年改名为五十铃汽车公司。该公司生产的汽车品种很多，是生产重型、轻型货车的主要厂家，是世界上最具规模及历史最悠久的商用汽车制造企业之一，主要产品有五十铃Rodeo皮卡，五十铃H系列中型卡车，五十铃N系列卡车。

8. 大发汽车（DAIHATSU）

大发汽车公司成立于1907年，公司总部设在日本大阪。不论在汽车还是在发动机方面，大发汽车公司以"小"见长，在小型发动机制造技术具有相当高的水平，处于世界领先地位。1983年研制出世界最小排量的0.993升三缸四冲程柴油发动机，突破了柴油机每缸排量需0.4升以上的技术限制，天津夏利即采用了大发的技术。目前丰田汽车公司占有大发的多数股份。

9. 富士重工汽车（SUBARU）

富士重工的前身是一间飞机制造所，1953年更名为富士重工业股份有限公司。富士赛车享有盛誉，1989年1月富士力狮跑车以平均223.345公里的时速，连续奔驰19天，同时刷新了10万公里竞速世界纪录，纪录保持多年未破。主要产品有四驱动轿车、微型车、轻型汽车和大客车，其中以四驱动轿车畅销世界，著名品牌有力狮和翼豹。